# Management Speak



Management gurus continue to exert tremendous influence over management thinking and strategy, not only through their published works, but more significantly via their live lectures on the international management lecture circuit. Research suggests that these public performances are critical to their continuing popularity and success, and that the most renowned gurus are all highly skilled in deploying a small range of persuasive communication techniques.

*Management Speak* examines the verbal and non-verbal communication techniques used by gurus to captivate their audiences and in the process establish and sustain their reputations as highly effective orators. It focuses on video recordings of live talks given by Tom Peters, Rosabeth Moss Kanter, Peter Senge and Gary Hamel, who are all renowned for their public performances and the impact they have had on organizational life.

Challenging and original, this text is indispensable reading for all those interested in finding out more about the influence of management gurus and the sources of spellbinding oratory more generally.

**David Greatbatch** is Special Professor at the University of Nottingham and Managing Director of Greatbatch Associates Ltd, an independent research and evaluation consultancy.

**Timothy Clark** is Professor of Organisational Behaviour at Durham Business School, Durham University.

# Management Speak

## Why we listen to what management gurus tell us

David Greatbatch and
Timothy Clark

Routledge
Taylor & Francis Group
LONDON AND NEW YORK

First published 2005
by Routledge
2 Park Square, Milton Park, Abingdon, Oxon OX14 4RN

Simultaneously published in the USA and Canada
by Routledge
270 Madison Ave, New York, NY 10016

*Routledge is an imprint of the Taylor & Francis Group*



Typeset in Sabon with Gill Sans by Book Now Ltd

Printed and bound in Great Britain by
TJ International Ltd, Padstow, Cornwall



*British Library Cataloguing in Publication Data*
A catalogue record for this book is available from the British Library

*Library of Congress Cataloging in Publication Data*
A catalog record for this book has been requested

ISBN 0–415–30622–1 (hbk)
ISBN 0–415–30623–X (pbk)

For Sallie and Penny
and our children
Emily and Olivia; Max and India
who teach us so much about effective communication
in our everyday lives

# Contents

# Tables

# Preface

Our purpose in this book is to enhance understanding of the management guru phenomenon by reporting the findings of an empirical study of the gurus and their work. In doing so, we focus on the ways in which leading management gurus communicate their ideas through live oratory and presentations. Although management gurus espouse very different ideas and adopt a variety of styles of speaking, they share the extraordinary ability to attract large audiences to their live performances on the international management lecture circuit. Our main concern is to lay bare the communication techniques that enable them to do this.

It is commonly recognized that effective public speaking is a special skill. Many people dread giving a public speech, fearing exposure to the audience's gaze and that their shortcomings as a speaker will cause them considerable social embarrassment. Despite the plethora of self-help books, few of us ever master the ability to design and deliver a truly captivating speech. Yet we can all recognize when we have heard an effective public speaker. We can be pretty certain that others will share our opinions as to who is an effective and ineffective speaker. In part we can ascertain this from the kind of audience response a speaker receives during and after their talk. This suggests that while we may be unable to successfully imitate accomplished orators, we are nevertheless implicitly aware of the methods that underlie the delivery of a stimulating rather than a tedious speech. As we shall discuss in this book, researchers have begun to identify the verbal and non-verbal techniques that speakers deploy in order to generate a positive response from the audience. But, as we highlight, research in this area has been focused primarily on political oratory. To what extent these skills and techniques are transferable to other contexts and situations is unclear. Those features that characterize successful political oratory are not necessarily acceptable in other contexts.

This book therefore contributes to debates on the nature of public speaking as well as those on the role and nature of management gurus. With respect to the former, it considers whether oratorical skills are universal regardless of the context within which a speech is given. In other words, is what we presently understand to be deployed and effective within the political sphere also applicable to the management community? What skills do we need to be an effective speaker in both contexts? In terms of the latter, it asks what are the verbal and non-verbal techniques used by gurus when giving a live talk. How do they successfully communicate their messages to audiences of managers so as to receive a positive response? Overall, this book asks what underpins effective oratory in this context?

# Acknowledgements

We are deeply indebted to the matchmaking skills of Christian Heath who recognized the complementarities between our respective research interests and brought us together.

The research reported in this book would not have been possible without a grant from the Economic and Social Research Council for the project titled 'Talk in training: the live and video recorded performances of management gurus' (Grant No. R000222860). We are especially grateful to BBC Worldwide, The Tom Peters Group and VideoArts, in addition to the numerous practitioners who gave their time and resources so generously to support our research. Thanks also to Catriona King for commissioning the book and to Emma Joyes for seeing it through and making it such an enjoyable experience.

David Greatbatch would like to thank Max Atkinson and John Heritage for providing him with the opportunity to work on their pioneering studies of political oratory in the 1980s. He would also like to thank Christian Heath, Robert Dingwall and especially John Heritage for their generous intellectual support over the last 20 years and for the numerous insights they have given him into the issues addressed in this book.

Timothy Clark would like to thank Robin Fincham, Graeme Salaman, Derek Pugh, Matthias Kipping, Brad Jackson, Alfred Kieser, Andrew Sturdy, Karen Handley, Karen Legge, Joanne Roberts, Mike Wright, Chris Wright, Stephanos Avakian, Stefan Heusinkveld and Eric Guthey for numerous thought-provoking conversations that have helped deepen and sharpen many of his ideas on the nature of management gurus. His thanks also go to Lars Engwall and the Creation of European Management Practice research group for generously supporting the development of some of this work. Finally, he is extremely grateful to Durham Business School, University of Durham for his study leave in late 2004 during which much of the writing for this book was done.

Chapter 1

# Management gurus

We live in a televisual and mediated age in which communication technologies continue to proliferate and privilege indirect communication. In spite of this, live oratory remains important and significantly influences our opinions about individuals in the media spotlight. One only has to think about the amount of interest in the live debates between the two presidential candidates. In a different vein, many people will remember the shock-waves sent through Westminster Abbey and beyond when the Earl of Spencer turned on the royal family during his funeral oration for his sister Diana in 1997. In politics live speeches can still be decisive. In June 2000, the UK Prime Minister, Tony Blair, was slow hand-clapped, jeered and booed for a speech he gave to the Women's Institute national conference. The speech was deemed too political for this non-political meeting. This incident was seen as symptomatic of the end of the long honeymoon period he had enjoyed since first becoming Prime Minister in 1997. In the following months his public standing fell dramatically as the press criticized him for being arrogant, overly concerned with spin and out of touch. In the run-up to the Labour Party Conference in September 2000 the newspapers were calling his keynote speech the most important of his career. The speech he delivered received an enthusiastic response from the delegates and a five-minute standing ovation. The following day the broadsheet newspapers were positively effusive as they hailed it a resounding success. By the end of 2000 his poll ratings had improved and in May 2001 he won a second election landslide. This conference speech was subsequently seen as the start of the very successful Labour General Election campaign and marked the resurgence in their popularity with voters. Tony Blair proved that, if a speaker can convince the people in the auditorium, and – crucially – impresses the journalists present, the climate of opinion can change.

These examples show that live oratory is still a powerful tool and remains an important source of the public's perception of a politician's image and popularity. New visual technologies rather than killing-off live political oratory have perhaps increased its importance as speakers and their messages are exposed to an audience of millions rather than thousands. Political speeches live on not just as single performances in the context in which they are given but, if they are recorded or broadcast, through their constant replaying on television. To a large extent, politicians from previous eras are remembered through the clips of their speeches that are shown to subsequent generations. Martin Luther King is forever associated with his 'I Have a Dream' speech. President Kennedy is remembered for his speech delivered at the Berlin Wall in which he declared 'Ich bin ein Berliner' (I am a donut). Similarly, Winston Churchill is remembered more for his war-time oratory rather than his actions as a peace-time Prime Minister.

The speeches of more recent politicians are subject to unprecedented levels of scrutiny as they are continually featured and analysed on the main news bulletins. Well-written and well-presented passages are noticed and replayed on television news programmes with the consequence that they reach a mass audience and sometimes capture their hearts and minds as they crystallize the public mood. Just as importantly for the speaker, the media audience is also reminded of their failures as gaffes and poorly received segments of their speeches are broadcast and rebroadcast repeatedly to the detriment of their public image. This means that a speaker can no longer control and restrict the audience response to just the people sitting in the auditorium. Although these speeches ostensibly retain a traditional format, their impacts have been widened from the immediate confines of the auditorium as they have become a significant input into news programmes. In the UK a party leader's speech at the annual party conference is a major media event broadcast live on television. Similarly, in the United States a President's inaugural speech or a candidate's acceptance of their party's nomination is also a significant event carried live on television. For the media audience, perceptions of how a speech is received at the time it was given can have crucial reputational consequences. Leading political figures, as perhaps never before, are therefore under enormous pressure to be skilled orators as they perform regularly in front of live audiences. In the political arena an individual's oratorical skill is often viewed as a proxy measure of their broader abilities. It is therefore unlikely that anyone could achieve or sustain a senior position without being a technically proficient orator. It should come as no surprise that leading politicians surround themselves with speechwriters to assist in the crafting of what they hope will be well-received and high-impact speeches. This is not confined to the contemporary period since Presidents as far back as Lincoln used speechwriters.

In this book we examine another group of highly skilled and influential speakers – management gurus. These individuals are portrayed as the outstanding creators and proselytisers of purportedly innovative management ideas and techniques. As we shall discuss later in this chapter, they partly communicate their ideas to the managerial audience through writing best-selling management books. Some of the most successful include *In Search of Excellence* (Peters and Waterman, 1982), *The Seven Habits of Highly Effective People* (Covey, 1989), *When Giants Learn to Dance* (Kanter, 1989), *The Fifth Discipline* (Senge, 1990) and *Re-engineering the Corporation* (Hammer and Champy, 1993). In addition, they disseminate their ideas on the international management lecture circuit. As perhaps the highest profile group of management speakers in the world, they use their lectures to build their personal reputations with audiences of managers. Many gain reputations as powerful orators and subsequently market recordings of their talks as parts of video-based management training packages. As the popularity of their book begins to wane their continued success on the international lecture circuit helps them to maintain their star status. Indeed, many gurus become better-known for their live performances than their books as they attract and sustain a mass live following.

Our purpose in this book is to contribute to emerging debates about the guru phenomenon by reporting the findings of a research project that developed an empirically-based understanding of gurus and their work. In doing so, we focus on their live oratory and presentations. Our main concern is to understand the intricacies of how management gurus communicate their ideas to live audiences. As we shall discuss later in this chapter, despite gurus having very different opinions on how to manage contemporary organizations, they share a number of common features. Critical is the extraordinary ability to convey their messages in live presentations to large audiences and in the process to captivate their audience members so that they feel enthused about the ideas they have just heard.

It is commonly recognized that effective public speaking is a special skill. Many people dread giving a public speech, fearing exposure to the audience's gaze and that their shortcomings as a speaker will cause them considerable social embarrassment. Despite the plethora of self-help books, few of us ever master the ability to design and deliver a truly captivating speech. Yet we can all recognize when we have heard an inspiring public speaker. We can be pretty certain that we will not be alone in our judgements, and that others will share our opinions as to who is an effective and ineffective speaker. In part we can ascertain this from the kind of audience response a speaker receives during and after their talk. This suggests that while we may be unable to successfully imitate accomplished orators, we are nevertheless implicitly aware of the methods that underlie the delivery of a stimulating rather than a tedious speech. As we shall discuss in this book, researchers have begun to identify the verbal and non-verbal techniques that speakers deploy in order to generate a positive response from the audience. But, as we highlight, research in this area has been focused primarily on political oratory. To what extent these skills and techniques are transferable to other contexts and situations is unclear. The earlier example of Tony Blair's speech to the Women's Institute suggests there are limitations. Those features that characterize successful political oratory are not necessarily acceptable in other contexts.

This book therefore contributes to debates on the nature of public speaking as well as those on the role and nature of management gurus. With respect to the former, it considers whether oratorical skills are universal regardless of the context within which a speech is given. In other words, is what we presently understand to be deployed and effective within the political sphere also applicable to the management community? What skills do we need to be an effective speaker in both contexts? In terms of the latter, it asks what are the verbal and non-verbal techniques used by gurus when giving a live talk. How do they successfully communicate their messages to audiences of managers so as to receive a positive response? Overall, this book asks what underpins effective oratory in this context?

In the remainder of this chapter we begin by discussing the nature of management gurus and the reasons for their impact and popularity. We then provide an outline of the chapters to come.

## What is a management guru?

The term management guru has become the label of choice when commentators discuss influential management analysts and thinkers whether they are academics, consultants or practitioners. It has not been in use that long. A thorough search of a range of electronic databases reveals that its earliest use in newspapers was an article in the UK's *Sunday Times* in 1983. This coincides with the emergence of the guru phenomenon in North America in the early 1980s. With a few notable exceptions, such as Edward de Bono, Charles Handy and Kenichi Ohmae, most of the leading management gurus are American. Given this situation it is possible that certain features of American society support the development of management gurus and guru theory. These could include the focus on a dream, an idealized sense of possibility, the assumption that individuals are adaptable to a dynamic and changing future, and the relatively poor performance of American organizations in the face of (mainly) Japanese and south-east Asian competition, especially in the 1980s, and the subsequent emergence of a conviction of the inherent inadequacy, even dangers, of modern US management techniques and the need to (re)discover (borrow) previous principles of organization.

In the first academic study of management gurus Huczynski (1993) argued that 'guru theory' is the latest in a series of management idea families that have established themselves in the consciousness of academics, consultants and practitioners during the twentieth century. The earlier families included Bureaucracy, Scientific Management, Administrative Management, Human Relations, and Neo-Human Relations. Guru theory, although a diverse collection of apparently unconnected writings, involves the presentation of ambitious claims to transform managerial practice and organizational performance, often through the recommendation of an almost magical cure that 'reinterprets' the organization, its employees, their relationships, attitudes and behaviour. Much guru theory can be explained in terms of a project that contributes productively to the problems of organizational management, particularly the management of new forms of organization, by making the informal, the irrational, the intuitive, the emotional, the cultural, manageable. It is argued that these aspects can be legitimately and effectively managed. Peters and Waterman (1982), for example, are quite clear about this:

> what our framework has done is to remind the world of professional managers that 'soft is hard' . . . It has enabled us to say, in effect, 'All that stuff you have been dismissing for so long as the intractable, irrational, intuitive, informal organization can be managed.
>
> (Peters and Waterman, 1982: 11)

For Huczynski (1993: 38) guru theory is also distinctive because each idea 'relies for its authorization upon the individual who developed and popularized it'. The credibility of the idea is related to the perceived legitimacy of its author and this stems in large part from the source of their ideas. He therefore identifies three types of management guru: 1) 'academic gurus', 2) 'consultant gurus' and 3) 'hero managers'. The first group are generally located within a small number of world-renowned business schools (London, Harvard, Sloan, Stamford and so forth) and are exemplified by such people as Charles Handy, Gary Hamel, Rosabeth Moss Kanter, Michael Porter and Peter Senge. The second group is composed of independent advisers, writers and commentators and includes the likes of Peter Drucker, Michael Hammer and Tom Peters. The final group is comprised of successful and high-profile senior managers who either write a book based on their approach and experience of management or are featured in a book devoted to understanding their success. In the first type of book, managers are seeking to pass on their experiences to other managers. Notable examples include John Harvey Jones, Lee Iacocca, Luis Gerstner, Alfred P. Sloan, Donald Trump and Jack Welch. In the second type of book, a non-authorized biographer seeks to identify the factors accounting for their subject's success. The individuals featured in these books, such as Bill Gates and Steve Jobs, continue to manage and do not participate on the international management lecture circuit. Rather, their public speaking activities are limited to settings which promote their business activities rather than a management idea.

Despite differences in the backgrounds of individual gurus they nevertheless share three common characteristics: they are purveyors of management fashion, authors of best-selling books and accomplished orators. We discuss each of these features in the remainder of this section.

### *Guru ideas are fashionable*

Gurus are purveyors of management fashion. The popularity of their ideas waxes and wanes as they evolve through a series of discrete stages:

1 invention, when the idea is initially created;
2 dissemination, when the idea is initially brought to the attention of its intended audience;
3 acceptance, when the idea becomes implemented;
4 disenchantment, when negative evaluations and frustrations with the idea emerge; and
5 decline, or the abandonment of the idea (Gill and Whittle, 1993).

A plethora of empirical studies have examined the diffusion patterns of a range of fashionable guru-led discourses within the print media. Using citation analysis the number of references to a particular idea in a sequence of years are counted and plotted in order to identify the life cycle of a fashionable management idea.[1] The results of these studies demonstrate that the life-cycles of a number of fashionable management ideas are characterized by an initial period in which the frequency of citations increases, peaks and then declines; although the shapes of the curves for different ideas are not necessarily identical nor symmetrical (i.e. they do not necessarily rise and fall at the same rate) and vary between countries (Abrahamson and Fairchild, 1999; Benders and van Veen, 2001; Spell, 1999, 2001; Gibson and Tesone, 2001). Furthermore, while the life spans of recent management fashions are considerably shorter than those for ideas that came to prominence in earlier periods, their peaks are much higher. Carson *et al.* (2000: 1152) show that the period of time between the introduction of a fashionable management idea or technique and the peak in its popularity has fallen from a mean of 14.8 years in the 1950s to 1970s, to 7.5 years in the 1980s and to 2.6 years in the 1990s.[2]

Abrahamson (1996: 256) notes that management fashions are 'the product of a management-fashion-setting *process* involving particular management fashion setters – organizations and individuals who dedicate themselves to producing and disseminating management knowledge'. Management gurus are therefore part of a management knowledge arena, the other members of which are typically identified as consulting firms, business schools and management academics and publishers (see also Ernst and Kieser, 2002; Suddaby and Greenwood, 2001).[3] This group of knowledge entrepreneurs is concerned with the creation, fabrication and dissemination of ideas and techniques to the managerial audience. A range of commentators has noted that they are in a 'race' to sense consumers' emergent collective preferences for new techniques. They either thrive or falter depending on their ability to identify and satiate inchoate needs. They have to articulate why it is imperative that consumers should pursue certain organizational goals and why their particular technique offers the best means to achieve these goals (Abrahamson, 1996; Kieser, 1997). Gurus' success is therefore dependent on their ability to create a shared sense of which management techniques are state-of-the-art and are likely to meet the most immediate needs of the managerial audience.

### *Best-selling books*

Gurus are the authors of best-selling management books. These books have perhaps been the publishing phenomenon of the last 20 years. Prior to the publication of *In Search of Excellence* management books were deemed unfashionable and a minority interest. They rarely sold in large quantities and never in the millions. There were modest hits which included, for example, *The Organization Man* (Whyte, 1957), *Parkinson's Law* (Parkinson, 1957), *My Years with General Motors* (Sloan, 1964) and *Management: Tasks, Responsibilities, Practices* (Drucker, 1974). But the sales generated by the best-sellers of the 1980s and 1990s were of a different order of magnitude to these earlier books. *In Search of Excellence* sold 122,000 copies in the first two months of publication. Within one year it had sold more copies than any other book except the *Living Bible* in 1972 and 1973. The book has sold more than five million copies world-wide. Stephen Covey's book *Seven Habits* spent four years on the *New York Times* best-seller list and has sold more than six million copies world-wide. Hammer and Champy's book *Re-engineering the Corporation* has sold over two and a half million copies to date and was for a time the 'management's world's most fashionable fad' (Lorenz, 1993).

The success of *In Search of Excellence*, and subsequently a number of other titles, has raised the profile of the genre as a whole and resulted in management books enjoying a more prominent position in bookshops and a broader readership. These books have become an essential companion for thousands of business travellers with the consequence that they are heavily promoted with floor-to-ceiling displays at airport bookshops. Indeed, they account for 10 per cent of sales at WH Smith's Heathrow concessions. The popularity of these books with business travellers has led one commentator to pejoratively term this area 'Heathrow management theory' (Burrell, 1989).

Best-selling books are of such importance to launching a guru and their ideas that some authors may have sought to artificially inflate their sales figures and in the process influence the best-seller lists. For example, in 1995 *Business Week* exposed an intricate scheme that manipulated the sales of Treacy and Wiersema's *The*

*Discipline of Market Leaders* (1995) to ensure that it entered the *New York Times* best-seller list. Employees of CSC Index, which had been the birthplace for Hammer and Champy's *Re-engineering the Corporation* (1993) and where the two authors worked, appeared to have spent at least $250,000 purchasing more than 10,000 copies of the book. In addition, *Business Week* claimed that CSC Index channelled corporate purchases of an additional 30,000 to 40,000 copies through selected bookstores with the intent of raising the book's profile on the *Times* list. These purchases were in small quantities from dozens of bookstores across America that went unnoticed but had an impact on the book's place on the *Times* list. The magazine also suggested that *Re-engineering Management*, the follow-up by CSC founder and chief executive James Champy to his earlier book *Re-engineering the Corporation*, was also pushed up the best-seller lists by careful bulk purchases.

A study of the production of best-selling management books by the authors (Greatbatch and Clark, 2002, 2003) indicates that book editors are key gatekeepers whose decisions can either facilitate or block the career of a would-be best-selling author and the progress of an idea with potential mass appeal. Publishers are concerned with identifying, producing and distributing ideas that are likely to have a mass appeal. In this respect, the role that book editors play in 'discovering' potential popular authors and ideas is similar to that of 'contact people' in other cultural industries. Publishing, film and music companies all employ people to locate new manuscripts, new film scripts and new singers. These people essentially go out into the field and act as scouts attempting to identify potential stars from the existing pool of talent which can then be signed up by their organizations.

Editors have a significant, if largely unseen, impact on the fashioning of management ideas in book form. They work closely with authors helping shape their ideas prior to publication. Given the difficulty in predicting shifts in consumer tastes, it is not possible to determine with any degree of certainty what is likely to be a best-seller. Publishers therefore minimize this uncertainty by producing books in accordance with rules about what has been successful in the past (Greatbatch and Clark, 2002, 2003). Editors view managers as being extremely busy people with a focus on the tangible and immediate and a tendency towards superficiality and short attention spans. They therefore aim to present the ideas in accessible forms that have two characteristics. The first is that they are easy to read and remember. This requires that the main elements of the ideas be reduced and simplified into pithy lists, acronyms, concepts, mnemonics, metaphors and stories that are immediately graspable, understood and assimilated. Second, the editors use forms that emphasize and demonstrate the practical relevance of the gurus' ideas. They need to be made vivid and concrete for the audience. Often this involves relating stories of how the gurus' ideas have been successfully implemented in many organizations. It is these conventions, based on their understandings of past successes and failures, which are conveyed to authors during the writing process. In this way publishers aim to produce a book that at least meets the expectations of the managerial audience, and hopefully exceeds them so that it becomes a best-seller.

### *Live presentations*

In addition to writing best-selling management books, management gurus disseminate their ideas through live presentations on the international management lecture circuit. As perhaps the highest profile group of management speakers in the world, they use their lectures to build their personal reputations with audiences of managers. Many gain reputations as powerful orators and subsequently market recordings of their talks as parts of video-based management training packages. The gurus' public performances are critical to their popularity and success, and generate a significant proportion of their income. Indeed, their appearance fees can dwarf their book royalties. A top management guru can earn several million pounds a year from speaking engagements. Given the importance of these events to the nature of guru activity it is hardly surprising to discover that in the 1980s one of the most influential gurus, Tom Peters, was taking up to 150 seminars a year and charging around $60,000 per appearance. More recently he has limited his public performances to between 50–60 seminars a year and is estimated to earn between $70,000–$90,000 for a day-long seminar. Other management gurus, such as Stephen Covey, Gary

Hamel, Michael Hammer, Rosabeth Moss Kanter, Kenichi Ohmae and Peter Senge, also give live presentations and charge similar appearance fees.

Since this aspect of guru work is the focus of this book we shall discuss the limitations of the previous approaches to management gurus' public performances in more detail in the next chapter. However, it should be noted that they have largely consisted of theoretical discussions which, using the work of Lewin (1951) and Sargant (1997), have depicted the gurus as experts in persuasive communication who seek to transform the consciousness of their audiences through powerful oratory (Huczynski, 1993; Clark, 1995; Clark and Salaman, 1996, 1998; Jackson, 1996, 2001, 2002). In this respect, their presentation style is likened to that of evangelical preachers. They are portrayed as emotionally charged performers, delivering their messages with huge amounts of energy and through threat and confrontation as they exhort their audiences to change their ways. Related to this, these studies explain the gurus' oratorical power in terms of their use of a range of rhetorical devices identified in the seminal work of Atkinson (1984a, 1984b) on political oratory (see also Heritage and Greatbatch, 1986), which are discussed in detail in Chapter 3. In addition, Clark and Salaman (1998) have sought to develop this explanation further by arguing that a major reason for the gurus' appeal to managers is their ability to tell compelling stories during their live presentations.

The notion that gurus are powerful orators and that the major factor accounting for this is an evangelic style underpinned by a narrow range of rhetorical techniques and vivid stories is central to the nascent literature on management gurus. While these studies provide important insights into the role and impact of gurus' oratory they have singularly failed to subject their live performances to detailed empirical research. Indeed, we are only aware of two previously published descriptions of these events (Oliver, 1998; Sharpe, 1984). Neither gives a systematic and empirically rigorous account of these events. Instead they rely solely on the authors' impressions as observers. Overall, the extant literature on gurus' live performances is based on a series of assertions rather than empirical evidence. Consequently, many questions remain to be answered with respect to how management gurus communicate their ideas and visions during their public lectures. For example, what presentational techniques do they use to communicate their messages and why? What style(s) of oratory do they use? Do they deploy the same devices that underpin effective political oratory? What forms of speaker–audience interaction occur during the gurus' lectures? How do audiences respond to the gurus' modes of presentation? Are management guru lectures replete with stories? If so, what type of stories are told and how frequently? The purpose of this book is to provide empirically grounded answers to these questions.

## Outline of the book

The book comprises six further chapters. In Chapter 2 we examine the role and significance of management gurus and review and critique the extant literature on management guru oratory. We then introduce the four management gurus (Tom Peters, Rosabeth Moss Kanter, Peter Senge and Gary Hamel) whose public performances are examined in this book and describe our database and methodology. In Chapter 3 we show how, despite using different styles of speaking, the four management gurus structure their messages in similar ways. First, when extolling the virtues of practices that the audience members are unlikely to be using and/or criticizing practices that they are likely to be using, the gurus are careful to avoid directly criticizing their audiences. Second, they use a relatively small number of rhetorical devices that are associated with persuasive speaking in general to package their messages. We also establish that when audience members collectively display their affiliation with the gurus, they do so predominantly by laughing. In Chapter 4, we show that whereas in political oratory applause is the main form of collective audience response, in these lectures it is laughter. There are very few incidents of applause in these lectures. We argue that audience laughter is not simply a spontaneous reaction to messages whose content is self-evidently humorous, but rather is 'invited' by the gurus through the use of a range of verbal and non-verbal practices. Each of these is discussed in detail in conjunction with analysis of illustrative extracts from the lectures. Mastery of these practices is critical because, as we show in

Chapter 5, the eliciting of audience laughter plays an important role with regard to the expression of group cohesion and solidarity during the gurus' lectures and, when used effectively, it heightens audience attentiveness and makes the gurus' messages more memorable. Consequently, we argue, the gurus' use of humour can play an important role in establishing the conditions necessary to win and retain 'converts' to their management theories. Chapter 6 focuses on storytelling. The notion that a key reason for the gurus' reputations as powerful orators is the stories they tell is prominent within the literature on management gurus. In this chapter we examine how management gurus project the onset of a story to the audience and the implications this has for audience attentiveness. We then consider how the stories are formulated in order to (1) illustrate their ideas and visions, (2) reinforce the authority of their knowledge and (3) create and enhance their 'star' status. In conclusion, in Chapter 7 we discuss the wider implications of this book's arguments and findings. In particular, we consider whether oratorical skills are universal regardless of the context within which a speech is given.

Chapter 2

# Live presentations

To date, the small, but growing, literature on management gurus has been guided by an overarching concern to understand the reasons for the apparently powerful impact of their ideas on managers. In a wide-ranging review of this literature Clark and Salaman (1998) identified three conventional explanations for the appeal of guru theory for managers. The first draws implicitly upon a psychoanalytical approach to leader–follower relations in that it argues that guru theory satiates managers' psychological tensions that arise from their incapacity to control a world that appears chaotic, unstable and increasingly uncertain. A second type of explanation argues that the popularity and impact of particular gurus' ideas is related to their ability to (re)frame their analyses of contemporary management problems and solutions in such a way that they resonate with and are in harmony with the expectations of their target audience. If they fail to convince their target audience of the plausibility and appropriateness of their ideas then they are very likely to be ignored. As Grint notes (1994, p. 193) 'for this "plausibility" to occur the ideas most likely to prevail are those that are apprehended as capturing the *zeitgeist* or "spirit of the times"'. Successful gurus are therefore seen as having a nose for the zeitgeist. The third, and final, type of explanation, and the one that is the focus of this book, argues that the success and impact of gurus' ideas is due to the form in which they are presented – their powerful public performances.

Despite this literature being dominated by a concern to understand the impact of gurus and their ideas on managers, to date the gurus themselves have only been studied in terms of the artefacts they produce. Previous research has either been entirely theoretical (e.g. Abrahamson, 1996; Clark and Salaman, 1996, 1998; Huczynski, 1993; Kieser, 1997), focused largely on textual analyses of the gurus' books (e.g. Furusten, 1999; Gerlach, 1996; Grint, 1994; Jackson, 2001), or comprised evaluations of the effectiveness of the change programmes they inspire (e.g. Watson, 1994; Fincham, 1999). Hence, although these studies purport to examine the work of management gurus they have nevertheless completely ignored the central character – the management guru. There is therefore a pressing need for the guru to be instated at the centre of an inquiry into their activities.

As we indicated in the previous chapter, this book fills this lacuna by conducting a detailed empirical analysis of the lectures of four management gurus: Tom Peters, Rosabeth Moss Kanter, Peter Senge and Gary Hamel. In this chapter we begin by reviewing critically the previous literature on guru public performances. Following this we introduce in more detail the management gurus featured in the book before discussing the data and the analytical approach adopted.

## Previous literature on guru live presentations

The gurus' public performances are critical to their popularity and success, and generate a significant proportion of their income. Indeed, their appearance fees can dwarf their book royalties. A top management guru can earn several million pounds a year from their speaking engagements. For example, Tom Peters is estimated to earn around \$6 million a year from his speaking activities. Other management gurus, such as Stephen Covey, Gary Hamel, Michael Hammer, Rosabeth Moss Kanter, Michael Porter and Peter Senge, also regularly give live presentations and charge appearance fees upwards of \$30,000 a talk. Crainer (1997: 197–201) argues that there are around fifty individuals on the international management lecture circuit that he terms 'global superstars' who can charge fees of this nature. He has estimated the total global market for guru performances to be a little under \$1 billion a year.

As we indicated earlier in Chapter 1, public perceptions of an individual are often related to their effectiveness as a public speaker.

Audiences are likely to be more questioning of gurus' pronouncements if they are conveyed in a manner that is perceived to be ineffective. It is not surprising therefore that a number of commentators have argued that management gurus' public performances are exercises in persuasive communication (e.g. Clark, 1995; Clark and Salaman, 1996; Huczynski, 1993). Indeed, to date, the main purpose of these events has been understood in terms of the conversion of the audience to the guru's way of thinking by restructuring managers' ways of thinking and in so doing to transform their consciousness.

Although previous accounts of gurus' live lectures do not refer to the enormous body of literature on religious conversion, there are obvious parallels. The notion of conversion employed in the guru literature is similar to Travisano's (1970: 594) oft quoted definition – 'a radical reorganization of identity, meaning, life'. This in turn is similar to Heirich's (1977: 674) notion of conversion as 'the process of changing a sense of root reality' or 'a conscious shift in one's sense of grounding'. A key point made in the literature on religious conversion is that it can take many forms. In contrast, the assumption in the literature on management guru performances is that conversion takes a single form. In a seminal article Lofland and Skonovd's (1981) identified six 'conversion motifs'. These refer to those 'aspects of conversion which are most memorable and orienting to the person "doing" or "undergoing" personal transformation – aspects that provide a tone to the event' (p. 374). According to Lofland and Skonovd's framework the conversion process pictured as occurring within the gurus' performances has a 'revivalist' motif. This form of conversion occurs at events which aim to enthral and uplift the audience. Participants experience a series of emotional highs as the sequence of elements build on one another with exhilarating momentum. In addition, they involve a range of actions aimed at generating and reinforcing group solidarity such as singing, chanting, clapping and hand-holding. This social contagion produces 'fear, guilt, and joy of such intensity that individuals may obediently go through the outward and inward methodology of a fundamentalist or evangelical conversion' (p. 381). At the centre of the event is the preacher orchestrating the activities and through their actions ensuring that the audience is 'swept into this performance of continual consensus' (Taylor, 1978: 154; quoted in Lofland and Skonovd, 1981: 381). The oratorical skills of the preacher are therefore critical in raising the emotional temperature of the event so that the audience enthusiastically participate. If these events are to be a success they require the preacher to be a persuasive public speaker.

According to Scheidel (1967) the aim of persuasive speaking is to 'modify a listener's beliefs and/or affects toward the proposition advanced by the speaker' (p. 57). He argues that persuasive speakers are seeking to change the attitudes, beliefs and value systems of audience members. These systems are the way in which we label, order and structure the complex and evolving world in which we live. However, these are not grounded in some kind of immutable truth since they have been invented not discovered. They 'exist in man rather than in nature' (Scheidel, 1967: 33). The boundaries and content of these categories may therefore change as we react to and evaluate different experiences. Hence, an essential feature of our attitudes, beliefs and value systems is their potential vulnerability to external influences. As a consequence, they can be modified, shaped and moulded through the clever manipulation of certain persuasive techniques. This is echoed by Huczynski (1993: 245) when he writes that: 'A realistic aim of the guru's persuasive communication is not that his ideas should necessarily and immediately modify the *actions* of his audience, but that they should alter their *beliefs*, *attitudes* and *feelings* towards his suggestions.' He adopts Lewin's (1951) three-phase change model to develop an explanation for the power of gurus' lectures and applies it in the following way:

*Unfreezing*: This phase creates the conditions that are necessary if members of the audience are to change. It is a period in which the management guru seeks to 'soften up' their audience, to destabilize them, to make them indecisive, uncertain and self-questioning. In essence, they seek to disturb the taken-for-granted, unquestioned notions, mind sets and recipes that the members of the audience bring to the event. This depends on rousing strong emotions in their audience. Drawing upon Sargant's (1997) seminal analysis of the psychological processes of brain-washing and conversion, he argues that the guru is more likely to be successful at achieving change if they 'can first induce some degree of nervous tension or stir up sufficient feelings of anger or anxiety to secure the person's undivided attention and possibly increase his suggestibility' (p. 82). He illustrates this using the example of the eighteenth-century preaching style of John Wesley, one of the founders of Methodism. As the following passage shows, Wesley threatened his audiences with eternal hellfire if they did not change:

> Wesley would create high emotional tension in his potential converts. He found it easy to convince large audiences that a failure to achieve salvation would necessarily condemn them to hellfire for ever and ever. The immediate acceptance of an escape from such a ghastly fate was then very strongly urged on the ground that anybody who left the meeting 'unchanged' and met with a sudden accident before he accepted this salvation, would pass straight into the fiery furnace.
>
> (Sargant, 1997: 88)

Similarly, Huczynski (1993) argues that management gurus begin their presentations by creating disequilibrium through challenging audience members' normative world-views and thereby heightening their levels of anxiety and emotional stress. This, he suggests, increases the suggestibility of the audience to new ideas and creates the conditions for conversion.

*Changing*: Huczynski (1993: 257) suggests that management gurus achieve changes in managers' attitudes, beliefs and values through a combination of 'push-and-pull factors'. The major push factor concerns the encouragement of potential converts to identify with a new idea. Again drawing upon the work of Sargant (1997), he suggests that this is achieved by contrasting the old and the new in such a way that the new is made more attractive. He writes of John Wesley that:

> One must also provide an escape from the induced mental stress. Hellfire is presented only as the result of *rejecting* the offer of eternal salvation won by faith. Emotionally disrupted

> by this threat, and then rescued from everlasting torment by a total change of heart, the convert is now in a state to be helped by dwelling upon the complementary gospel of Love.
>
> (ibid.: 91)

Gurus, it is argued, similarly play on the uncertainty in the manager's mind created by the initial onslaught to their taken-for-granted ways of thinking. They juxtapose the 'old' and the 'new' in such a way that the 'new' undermines the 'old'. As a consequence, managers feel less certain and committed to their existing (i.e. 'old') and possibly cherished ways of thinking than before their attendance at the event. The 'new' offers a path towards certainty and apparent redemption; two goals sought by many managers. Those who may think of deviating and returning to 'old' recipes and ways of doing things are aware that severe penalties may accompany their actions since the contrast stresses the many deficiencies of the 'old'. Furthermore, conversion to the 'new' and rejection to the 'old' is often presented as a matter of extreme urgency. The ultimate scenario for failing to adopt the 'new' is organizational failure. This creates a sense of urgency that increases the levels of anxiety and suggestibility among the audience members. An example of this is a segment from a speech given by Tom Peters to an audience of pub and restaurant managers in which he ridiculed General Motors' numbers-driven management approach. Caulkin writes:

> GM knew so much, sneered Peters, that it ignored half the population: it didn't realise that women drove cars, too. As the audience titters comfortably, Peters stuck the knife in: 'Why the f*** are you laughing? Your company's only just realized that women go into pubs.'
>
> (Caulkin, 1977)

The pull factors relate to the 'release in tension which follows the acceptance of the new position; they value the comfort of having re-established their cognitive balance (after the unpleasant cognitive dissonance experience while being torn between the old and new views)' (Huczynski, 1993: 257). Having had their taken-for-granted mind sets battered, questioned and undermined there is comfort in the new reassuring world being offered by the guru. Accepting the new leads to new-found confidence. Conversion ensures that the anxiety, indecision and self-questioning associated with the old way of thinking reduces and becomes a distant memory to be replaced by comfort and balance.

*Refreezing*: According to Huczynski (1983: 265) the next stage of the process is to reinforce and permanently fix the change. The focus is 'upon the fixing of the persuasive influence' (Scheidel 1967: 76). This occurs after the completion of the management guru's performance. Once the event has come to an end there is the danger that the audience members will revert to their old mind sets and ways of thinking. The actions of the guru that led to changes in managers' ideas and categories occur during the persuasive speaking event. Once the guru performance is at an end and the members of the audience have left the auditorium the communication of the message finishes and their persuasive influence diminishes. If the managers' attendance at the event is to have a long-lasting impact the audience members must learn (i.e. internalize) some aspects of their restructured attitude, belief and value systems. Learning theory suggests that behaviour patterns that are rewarded tend to be repeated. As a consequence, a follow-up procedure is vital if recent converts are to remain steadfast in their commitment to their new-found beliefs. If this does not happen the speaker and the message will become separated with the consequence that the guru's influence on their audience will dissipate. Gurus may attempt to overcome this by selling copies of videos of their performances, giving away free copies of their books and offering follow-up consultancy packages. The key is to maintain some kind of contact between the guru and the audience beyond and between performances.

This description of the unfolding nature of gurus' live performances and the reasons for their impact on audiences is detailed and has been very influential. Indeed, it has become an unquestioned caricature that dominates present understandings of these events. As we mentioned earlier, gurus' live lectures are repeatedly portrayed as equivalent to evangelical religious revivalist meetings.

They are evangelists who pass among their flock. Their talks are replete with parables about companies and individuals that saw the light and were saved. They are presented as whipping their 'congregations' into a state of hysterical compliance with their message by engaging in hellfire preaching (see for example, Baur, 1994; Crainer, 1997; Micklethwait and Wooldridge, 1996; *The Economist*, 1994). Their approach and style is therefore seen as identical to that of Billy Graham, Martin Luther King and, from an earlier period, John Wesley. Their style of performing is thus characterized as comprising some, if not all, of the following elements:

- A powerful physical presentation with a great deal of restless energy.
- Demonic energy, arms flailing, sweating face, a hoarse voice and near exhaustion.
- High levels of commitment and passion which generate an intensity of experience for audience and presenter.
- Challenge, threat, confrontation. The audience is not allowed simply to sit and receive information (i.e. to spectate passively). It is brought into the event by direct challenge and attack.
- The lectures are not bland, calm, neutral presentations of options and possibilities; rather they are guided by conviction and certainty. The performer will show, *must* show, absolute certainty and conviction. The performer must reveal to the members of the audience 'the road to the centre of the world: the hole in the sky through which he can fly up to the highest heaven, or the aperture through which he can descend to the underworld' (Eliade, 1987: 205). If they falter, the audience falters. They must believe in themselves so that the audience believe in them.
- There is the presence of danger, risk and surprise. It's not safe. The audience might be exposed, caught out at any moment. There will be threat and danger for all parties – presenter and audience alike. Things could go wrong. It might be embarrassing; in fact it almost certainly will, anything may happen; but they will get away with it – but only just.
- The message is posed in riddles, in dilemmas, in mysteriously

> gained insights that leave the audience impressed by the performer's knowledge of them and their experience. The presenter 'knows' them, 'knows' their problems, 'knows' their subterfuges and tricks. They are open to the presenter and therefore susceptible to persuasion.

In addition, these studies explain the gurus' oratorical power in terms of their use of the rhetorical devices identified in the seminal work of Atkinson (1984a, 1984b) on political oratory (see also Heritage and Greatbatch, 1986).

Except for the authors' work, we are only aware of two previously published descriptions of these events. Oliver (1998) provides a brief description of a seminar given by Eli Goldratt, the co-author of *The Goal* (Goldratt and Cox, 1982). In this he elaborates his 'theory of constraints'. Oliver notes that:

- Goldratt gave what appeared to be an improvised talk in that he stressed from the outset that he had not pre-prepared slides or notes.
- At one point during this event he sought to draw-out a contrast between the 'cost' and 'throughput' worlds. His aim was to show the key deficiencies of the 'cost' world and how these would become redundant once the 'throughput' world was embraced. Furthermore, one world was understood as 'bad' and the other as 'good'. He then attempted to show through a series of exercises that most of the managers in the room were entrenched in the 'bad' 'cost' world and that: 'It will not be easy to move from a cost world to the throughput world. We have to throw away much of what we have learnt over the last thirty years . . . We've met the enemy. It's us' (p. 21). He thus juxtaposed the 'old' and the 'new' in such a way that the 'new' was presented as more attractive than the 'old'.
- Finally, we learn that Goldratt sought to convince the audience of the practical benefits of his ideas by introducing 'a large coloured gentleman to the audience . . . The gentleman introduced himself as Emerson, and then proceeded to describe what Goldratt's ideas had done for his company' (p. 20).

Oliver concludes by arguing that this episode is notable, in part, because of 'the imagery of religious conversion that was very much in evidence throughout the seminar. This was embodied in Goldratt's style of presentation, in his dress, and as the seminar progressed by the way the audience responded to him' (p. 25).

In the second account Sharpe (1984) very briefly outlines a number of features of a performance given by John Fenton, who runs master classes in sales skills. The author tells us that the audience numbered 600. Fenton nevertheless held their attention since the article notes that many of those who attended 'wrote furiously for 5 hours' while 'others sat attentively' (p. 15). We learn nothing about the nature of Fenton's message. But like Goldratt, Fenton's presentational style is characterized as 'an American style evangelical approach' (p. 16).

As we have shown, the notion that gurus are powerful evangelical orators is central to the existing literature that has examined their activities. While these studies provide important insights into the role and impact of gurus' oratory their live performances have not previously been subject to detailed empirical research. Consequently, it is replete with unfounded assumptions with respect to the gurus' dominant speaking style, the oratorical techniques they employ, the nature of speaker–audience interaction and the forms of audience response. In this respect, guru speeches are seen to be identical to those given by politicians at party conferences and other major political events. This is a critical assumption that we will begin to explore in Chapter 3 and then throughout the book. As will become apparent, management guru lectures have more in common with those that take place in university lecture theatres or at organizational conferences than church and political meetings. There are a number of key contextual differences that impinge on the nature of speaker–audience interaction. We cannot therefore assume that the oratorical skills necessary to succeed in one arena are transferable to the other.

A further weakness of the extant literature is that it assumes a simplistic and one-way conception between the guru and their managerial audiences. Gurus are portrayed as the dominant, initiating partners who exploit the naiveté and vulnerability of their audience of managers by selling them glib promises, and converting them to their way of thinking through their persuasive rhetoric and dazzling performances. Managers, on the other hand, are conceived largely as passive, docile consumers of gurus' ideas and recommendations, inherently vulnerable to gurus' blandishments, anxiously searching for reassurance and support, and looking desperately for new ideas.

The lack of detailed analyses of the interaction between gurus and their audiences means that many questions remain to be answered with respect to how management gurus disseminate their ideas on the international management lecture circuit. For example, what types of message do they communicate? What presentational techniques do they use to communicate their messages and why? What styles of speaking do they employ? What forms of speaker–audience interaction occur during the gurus' lectures? How do audiences respond to their messages? What impact do audience members' immediate reactions have on the gurus' modes of presentation?

## The management gurus featured

In this book we seek to answer the questions listed above and overcome the limitations of previous research just noted through detailed analysis of video recordings of public lectures given by four leading management gurus: Tom Peters, Rosabeth Moss Kanter, Peter Senge and Gary Hamel. These gurus are each renowned for their public performances and represent a range of popular ideas that have had a major impact on organizational life in the last twenty or so years. Indeed, as Table 2.1 shows, they each feature in the upper reaches of different rankings of influential management thinkers.

### *Tom Peters*

Tom Peters is widely regarded as the Ur-guru in that he is recognized as the creator of the modern management guru phenomenon (Crainer, 1997; Furnham, 1996; *The Economist*, 1994). Before joining McKinsey in 1974 he had worked in the Pentagon, in Washington for the Office of Management and Budget, served in

*Table 2.1* Rankings of the influence of four management gurus

| | *Accenture (2003)*[1] | *The Thinkers 50 (2003)*[2] |
|---|---|---|
| | *Ranking* | *Ranking* |
| Tom Peters | 2 | 3 |
| Rosabeth Moss Kanter | 11 | 9 |
| Peter Senge | 5 | 14 |
| Gary Hamel | 7 | 4 |

1 The overall ranking is based on the sum of ranks for each individual in three separate groupings: (1) Web hits using the Google search engine; (2) media mentions using three Lexis/Nexis database between 1997–2002; and (3) scholarly citations in the SSCI indices between 1997–2002. The top ten were Michael Porter, Tom Peters, Robert Reich, Peter Drucker, Peter Senge, Gary S. Becker, Gary Hamel, Alvin Toffler, Hal Varian, Daniel Goleman.

2 This is based on a wide-ranging survey which asks respondents to list 'Who is the most important living management thinker?' The top ten were Peter Drucker, Michael Porter, Tom Peters, Gary Hamel, Charles Handy, Philip Kotler, Henry Mintzberg, Jack Welch, Rosabeth Moss Kanter and Jim Collins.

Vietnam and obtained a master's degree in civil engineering from Cornell University. He came to prominence in 1982 by co-authoring *In Search of Excellence* with Robert Waterman. This book was an instant hit and has become viewed as the book that launched the guru phenomenon. The dimensions for excellence emerged from an investigation of the practices of successful companies within the strategy consultancy McKinsey. Although 75 companies were originally included in the research, 13 European companies were omitted 'because they do not represent a fair cross-section of European companies' (Peters and Waterman, 1982: 19). Eventually 43 companies that were determined to have been industry leaders for 20 years (1960–1980) and to have been innovative qualified for inclusion. On the basis of their research they identified eight attributes common to most of these so-called excellent companies. Briefly summarized these attributes are:

1 *A bias for action* is a preference for getting on with it and doing something rather than allowing organizational processes to cause delays.

2 *Close to customers* is showing a concern for, and interest in, the wishes of their customers.
3 *Autonomy and entrepreneurship* relates to fostering and valuing innovation and nurturing champions.
4 *Productivity through people* recognizes the importance of employees and emphasizing this in involvement programmes and activities designed to reinforce in employees the importance of their contribution to the success of the organization.
5 *Hands-on value-driven* means that senior executives promote a strong corporate culture and remain in close contact with core business activities.
6 *Stick to the knitting* implies that successful companies stay close to the businesses they know best and avoid the temptation of becoming collections of unconnected businesses.
7 *Simple for, lean staff* suggests companies maintain a simple organization and small head office staff.
8 *Simultaneous loose–tight properties* emphasizes strong core values which permit considerable flexibility to those who adhere to them.

In 1985 Peters co-authored a follow-up book, *A Passion for Excellence* (Peters and Austin, 1985). This addressed the question of how to put the principles of *In Search of Excellence* into practice. Without denying the validity of the eight attributes, emphasis was placed on the four elements that were considered to be the most important: concern for customers, innovation, attention to the people in the organization and, above all, leadership. The emphasis on the latter element was new, but Peters claimed it had been embedded in the original book. Peter's third book, *Thriving on Chaos* (1987) departs even further from the approach of *In Search of Excellence*. The opening sentence provocatively asserts: 'There are no excellent companies.' This message now emphasizes the need for constant, rapid change to survive in a rapidly changing world. He has continued this theme in a number of subsequent books such as *Liberation Management* (1992), *In Pursuit of Wow!* (1994) and *The Tom Peters Seminar: Crazy Times Call for Crazy Organizations* (1994).

Since leaving McKinsey in late 1981 he has become the leading performer on the international management lecture circuit.

### *Rosabeth Moss Kanter*

Rosabeth Moss Kanter is Ernest E. Arbuckle Professor of Business Administration at Harvard Business School, and between 1989–1992 was Editor of *Harvard Business Review*. Her undergraduate studies were in sociology at the female academy Bryn Mawr. She received her PhD from the University of Michigan and has subsequently taught at the universities of Yale, Brandeis and Harvard, where she has been based since 1986. She is the author or co-author of over 16 books of which *The Change Masters* (1985), *When Giants Learn to Dance* (1989) and *World Class: Thriving Locally in the Global Economy* (1995) have been her most influential (Puffer, 2004). In *The Change Masters* she contrasts 'change resisters' with 'change masters'. Kanter's principal finding is that firms prone to innovate have an 'integrative' approach to problems and a willingness to challenge established practices; to judge a course of action by a vision of the future rather than by the accepted ways of the past. Firms less likely to innovate were typically 'segmentalist' in approach, compartmentalized by department and unable to see problems as a whole. Throughout the book she argued that the key to corporate renaissance was 'participation management' or empowerment – which made possible the mechanisms by which individuals could contribute their ideas. In integrative companies the contribution of individuals to the corporate success is valued. In *When Giants Learn to Dance* she extends this philosophy to the future shape and character of the globally competitive corporation. She argues for the need to move to the 'post-entrepreneurial' corporation which, to paraphrase her, has the power of an elephant but is as nimble as a dancer. In *World Class* she examines how the global economy and expansion of consumer choice is transforming companies of all sizes and the communities in which they operate. One of her most recent books has the rather contrived title, *Evolve: Succeeding in the Digital Culture of Tomorrow* (2001).

She is the recipient of numerous awards and honorary degrees. She founded Goodmeasure in 1977 with Barry Stein. This offers consultancy services, training, planning and implementing business meetings and research and analysis. It also has a Speaker's Service called Voices of Experience. She is the top attraction. Apart from being a very highly-regarded academic she is an active supporter of women in management. She is a founding committee member of the International Women's Forum. She is a frequent and highly respected speaker on the international lecture circuit delivering keynote speeches and sessions at meetings of trade associations, civic groups, and (inter)national conventions.

### *Peter Senge*

Peter Senge is a Senior Lecturer at the Massachusetts Institute of Technology (MIT) and Chairperson of the Society for Organizational Learning (SoL), a global community of corporations, researchers and consultants dedicated to the 'interdependent development of people and their institutions'. He graduated in engineering from Stanford, but has been at MIT since 1970. He is the author of *The Fifth Discipline: The Art and Practice of the Learning Organization* (1990). The major contribution of this book was to identify five 'component technologies' that when combined underpin a 'true' learning organization. The 'five disciplines' are:

1 Personal mastery is the principle of an individual's commitment to continuous and lifelong learning which supports 'expanding the ability to produce the results we really want' (p. 142).
2 Mental models uncover 'deeply held internal images of how the world works' which in the process assist with 'surfacing, testing and improving our internal pictures of how the world works' and result in the development of new understandings (p. 174).
3 Building shared vision refers to creating pictures about the future that are compelling and result in a commitment to a shared goal. These 'create a sense of commonality that permeates the organization and gives coherence to diverse activities' (p. 206).
4 Team learning means that there is alignment in teams with the consequence that 'a commonality of direction emerges, and individuals' energies harmonize' (p. 234). This results in 'a

commonality of purpose, a shared vision, and understanding of how to complement one another's efforts' (p. 234).

5 Systems thinking is defined as 'a framework for seeing interrelationships rather than things, for seeing patterns of change rather than static "snapshots"' (p. 68).

The success of this book has established him as the world's leading authority on the learning organization. In *The Fifth Discipline Fieldbook: Strategies and Tools for Building a Learning Organization* (Senge *et al.*, 1994) he presents practical tools for applying the five disciplines in organizations wishing to create their own learning organization. More recently in *The Dance of Change: The Challenges to Sustaining Momentum in Learning Organizations* (1999) he tackles the problems of sustaining learning in organizations over a long time. He remains a much respected and in-demand management speaker.

### *Gary Hamel*

Originally a hospital administrator he changed career in 1978 to study for a PhD in international business at the University of Michigan where he met his initial collaborator C.K. Prahalad. They co-authored *Competing for the Future* (1994). This is currently the best-selling book ever on strategy. In it Hamel and Prahalad took issue with the then prevailing view of strategy, which focused largely on external competitive pressures. Businesses competed with the primary goal of winning market share from opponents and were guided in their strategic planning and decision-making by what competitors were doing or might do. Hamel and Prahalad argued that this was misguided. Rather than look at competitors, businesses ought to focus on their own strengths and on what their customers wanted. Aligning capabilities with the needs of customers was, they argued, the key to competitive success. Core competencies are sometimes defined as unique skills or attributes: 'what a company is good at'. Core competencies are not simply what a company values about itself; they are what customers value about the company. Any definition must begin with the customer's point of view; any attribute that cannot be seen to be desired by the customer is not a core competency.

He subsequently authored *Leading the Revolution* (2002) in which he urged companies to innovate and be revolutionary, turning themselves into 'relentless innovators' constantly seeking to exceed customer demands and thus staying ahead of competitors.

In addition to these books he has written over ten articles in *Harvard Business Review*, four of which received the McKinsey Prize for excellence. He is also the most reprinted author in the history of the *Harvard Business Review*. *The Economist* has referred to him 'the world's reigning strategy guru'. He is presently Visiting Professor of Strategic and International Management at the London Business School, a post he held full-time between 1983–1993. On leaving LBS he moved back to California to be located near Silicon Valley, which he described as 'a very good vantage point to see the future coming'. Following the success of *Competing for the Future*, in 1995 he co-founded the consultancy Strategos Inc. This offers services related to his ideas of 'competitive innovation', 'core business renewal', 'core competencies' and 'strategic resilience'. With his rapid-fire and challenging style of presentation he now rivals Tom Peters as the most sought-after conference and seminar speaker. He is reported to earn as much as $150,000 for two days work. He spends much of the year travelling all over the world and typically gives a speech once a week.

## Data and methodology

The video recordings of the gurus' public lectures are drawn from the following commercially produced training packages (the abbreviations in parentheses are those referred to in extracts in subsequent chapters):

> Tom Peters – *Tom Peters Experience 1 & 2 (TPE 1+2)*, *Thriving on Chaos 1–3 (TOC 1–3)* and *Service with Soul (SwS)*;
>
> Rosabeth Moss Kanter – *Managing Change (MC)*, *The Great Corporate Balancing Act Part 1 and 2 (GCBA 1 and 2)* and *Lessons in Leadership (LinL)*;

Peter Senge – *The Fifth Discipline and the Infrastructures of a Learning Organisation (FD)*, *The Knowledge-Building Process: The Important Role of Learning Communities (KBD)*; and *Creating Transformational Knowledge (CTK)*;

Gary Hamel – *Lessons in Leadership (LinL)*.

The videos involving Peters and Moss Kanter combine footage of the two gurus lecturing with case studies and interviews concerning organisations that are mentioned in the gurus' lectures. The videos involving Senge and Hamel include complete performances. The 20 hours of video material contain approximately 15 hours of the gurus lecturing to audiences of managers, consultants and trainers.

In Chapters 3 and 4 the data are analysed using the approach and findings of conversation analytic (CA) research into public speaking (e.g. Atkinson 1984a, 1984b; Clayman, 1992, 1993; Heritage and Greatbatch, 1986; McIlvenny, 1996). CA research involves detailed, qualitative analysis of audio and video recordings of naturally occurring social interactions (Atkinson and Heritage, 1984; Boden and Zimmerman, 1991; Heritage, 1995; Pasthas, 1995; Zimmerman, 1988). CA research does not entail the formulation and empirical testing of a priori hypotheses. Rather, it uses inductive search procedures to identify regularities in verbal and/or non-verbal interaction. The objective is to describe the practices and reasoning that speakers use in producing their own behaviour and in interpreting the behaviour of others. Analysis emerges from the orientations and understandings that parties unavoidably display to each other during their interactions.

In locating and analysing recurring patterns of action and interaction, CA researchers repeatedly replay audio and or video recordings of naturally occurring interactions, carefully transcribing the events. The transcripts capture not only what is said, but also various details of speech production, such as overlapping talk, pauses within and between utterances, stress, pitch and volume. They may also track visual conduct such as gestures, facial expressions and gaze direction. These transcripts facilitate the fine-grained analysis of the recordings, enabling researchers to reveal and analyse tacit, 'seen but unnoticed' (Garfinkel, 1967) aspects of human conduct that would otherwise be unavailable for systematic study. Extracts from transcripts are included in research reports as exemplars of the interactional phenomena that are being investigated. A glossary of the transcription symbols used in this book is detailed in the Appendix on pages 139–140.

Although CA began with the study of ordinary conversation, it has been increasingly applied to other forms of interaction including medical consultations, broadcast interviews, calls for emergency assistance, organisational meetings, proceedings in small claims courts, family mediation sessions, psychiatric intake interviews and, as we shall see in this book, political oratory (e.g. Atkinson, 1984b; Boden, 1994; Clayman and Heritage 2003; Drew and Heritage, 1992; Maynard, 1984). A number of researchers have also extended its principles to the study of visual conduct (e.g. Goodwin, 1981; Heath, 1986; Heath and Luff, 2000). Despite its name, CA is a generic approach to the study of social interaction.

In building on the findings reported in Chapters 3 and 4, Chapter 5 moves away from a strictly CA perspective in order to consider the content of the messages that the gurus convey through the use the presentational techniques identified by our CA research. Ultimately, this allows us to reveal yet another layer of presentational techniques used by the gurus – techniques which are critical to understanding their success as management speakers. Chapter 6 also departs from a purely CA perspective in order to examine the gurus' use of stories, which, as noted above, has been identified as key to understanding how they gain reputations as powerful orators. Thus, although this chapter draws heavily on the CA literature on storytelling, it departs from a CA perspective in that it does not focus on the ways in which the gurus' stories emerge on a moment-by-moment basis within speaker–audience interaction. Unfortunately, it was not possible to do this because the video recordings generally focus on *either* the speaker *or* the audience and thus do not allow one to examine how the gurus adapt their stories to audience behaviours such as smiling, frowning, signs of restlessness, and the like. In the light of this, we had no option but to adopt a speaker-centred approach to the analysis of this important phenomenon.

## Conclusion

In this chapter we have developed our critique of the extant literature on management gurus and their public performances. We have argued that this literature is primarily concerned with developing conceptual understandings of management gurus and in conducting detailed analyses of their books. For whatever reason it has failed to empirically examine the work of the gurus themselves and, in particular, their public presentations. Following this we gave a brief pen portrait of the career and key ideas for each of the four management gurus that are the focus of this book. Finally, we discussed the nature of the dataset and the methods we have employed to analyse it.

Our method involves painstaking analysis of publicly available video recordings of the gurus' lectures. A number of organizations market videos of performances by Tom Peters, Rosabeth Moss Kanter and Peter Senge. In contrast recordings of Gary Hamel are very limited. Hence, we are only able to analyse one of his lectures. In the chapters that follow we shall illustrate our key arguments and points with extracts taken from these video recordings. The speech extracts discussed in Chapters 3–5 have been transcribed in accordance with a system evolved by Gail Jefferson (see Atkinson and Heritage, 1984) and outlined in the Appendix; however those examined in Chapters 5 and 6 have been transcribed using a less detailed orthography (unless they have been examined in the preceding CA chapters). This reflects the shift away from a CA perspective in Chapters 5 and 6. Even when the CA transcription system is used, we do not claim that the transcripts capture all the particularities of a video recording, nor that a transcript should be considered as a literal representation of the talk being analysed. Rather, they are designed to capture those particular features of the talk that are the focus of analysis and as such attempt to include as much relevant detail as possible. Our attempt is to balance the need for a certain amount of detail while making the material accessible to readers unfamiliar with this system. In this way we hope that the reader will obtain a flavour for the speakers and talks being analysed.

Chapter 3

# Packaging the message

We have established that management gurus are often portrayed as experts in persuasive communication who seek to transform the views of their audiences through powerful oratory (e.g. Clark and Salaman, 1996; Huczynski, 1993; Jackson 1996, 2001, 2002). As we noted in the previous chapter, the 'powerful oratory' of management gurus is commonly explained in two interrelated ways. Some observers suggest that the gurus adopt an evangelical style of speaking; while others explain the gurus' oratorical power in terms of their use of the rhetorical devices that Atkinson (1984a, 1984b) examined in his studies of political oratory. Unfortunately, in contrast to Atkinson's work, the literature on management guru oratory does not involve detailed analysis of video recordings of naturally occurring speeches. Accordingly, there is an implicit and unwarranted assumption that the styles of speaking used by evangelical preachers and the presentational techniques used by politicians are also those used in management guru oratory, and in the same proportion. In this chapter, we begin to explore these propositions by examining how the gurus present their messages. The chapter is structured around a consideration of three interrelated issues. We begin by describing the main features of each guru's speaking style. The key issue we wish to highlight is that there are important differences. They cannot all be characterized as evangelical speakers. Following this, we turn to consider how gurus convey messages without directly criticizing their audiences. We show how the gurus, by deflecting potential criticism away from the audience members, create an affiliative atmosphere in their lectures.

Finally, we describe the seven rhetorical devices identified with the elicitation of applause in political oratory. A central issue for subsequent chapters is whether these devices are the key to understanding the success of the gurus on the international management lecture circuit.

## Styles of speaking

In the previous chapter we have established that gurus' live lectures are frequently portrayed as equivalent to evangelical religious revivalist meetings. However, this characterization is far from satisfactory because in reality management gurus do not adopt a uniform style of speaking. In this section we describe the range of speaking styles they adopt by examining each of the four gurus that are the focus of the present study.

### *Tom Peters*

Tom Peters perhaps comes closest to the evangelical style that is mistakenly attributed to management gurus in general (see pp. 22–23). Peters often adopts an aggressive and hectoring tone. He peppers his lectures with colloquialisms, profanities and hyperbole, uses exaggerated facial expressions and gestures, volume and pitch as he regales his audiences. Interestingly, in contrast with the other gurus examined in this study, he keeps audience members under constant surveillance, and is fond of gazing at individual audience members for prolonged periods of time, especially as he delivers key messages. Indeed, he is known to prefer what is termed the 'cocktail' arrangement (round tables with 10–15 people seated on each) for the auditoria in which he speaks. In this arrangement there is no stage and so he is free to roam the room and maintain direct contact with individual members of the audience. However, Peters engages in sustained interaction with his audiences, regardless of whether he is walking among then or speaking from a stage. It is perhaps not surprising therefore that members of his audiences often look decidedly uncomfortable as Peters adopts a hectoring/aggressive style and looks directly at them, searching out the gaze of individual audience members. Many of these characteristics are exemplified in the following extract.

**Extract 3.1 – "fair day's work for a fair day's pay" [TOC 3: 1.02.16]**

Peters: Er:, and so everything is changing. (0.7) And the front line worker has a hell of a job in the front of him or her because he or she is totally responsible for re-educating themselves whether their company is enlightened or schmlos, (1.0) because only he or she who re-educates,=be they a vice president aged forty-one and a half (0,2) or a janitor aged seventeen and a half, (0.2) will survive. (1.0) The dumbest term that has ever been uttered in the English language, certainly for the future, is that obnoxious term [FAIR DAY'S WORK FOR A FAIR
[*Leans forward towards the audience, stares at individual audience member*
DAY'S PAY

In this brief extract, Peters characteristically uses everyday language ("schmlos", "dumbest"), hyperbole ("The dumbest term that has ever been uttered") and a profanity ("Hell of a job"). He also shouts loudly ("FAIR DAY'S WORK FOR A FAIR DAY'S PAY") and stares directly at an individual audience member as he completes his message. Perhaps because Peters is regarded as the ur-guru his style is seen as the model for management gurus more generally. However, Peters' style is unusual in terms of its intensity, use of striking language and extreme physical actions (i.e. the movement of his arms, hands and head). So, in some important respects Peters is far from the norm. Rather than being viewed as the exemplar model for management gurus' speaking style, he should perhaps be considered exceptional.

## *Peter Senge*

Like Peters, Senge interacts with his audience. However, unlike Peters, he rarely gazes at individual audience members for prolonged periods of time; rather he interacts visually with the audience as a whole. Senge also uses a more elevated, academic style of speaking than does Peters, and frequently quotes other academics and philosophers, such as Kant and Searle, when articulating his theories. Indeed, Senge devotes long passages in his lectures to outlining the epistemological theory that underpins his views concerning the learning organisation. Senge also presents himself as part of a team of researchers rather than as an individual, an approach that is consistent with his views on organisational learning. Perhaps the most distinctive aspect of Senge's lectures, though, is his use of audience participation techniques. As we shall see later, all the gurus invite laughter; however, only Senge invites audiences to respond to questions either verbally or non-verbally (by raising their hands). When Senge invites verbal responses from audience members, he generally invites audience members to assist in describing a state of affairs on which he subsequently comments, as in the following example:

**Extract 3.2 – "Schoolroom" [FD: 1.05.20]**

Senge: I think the practice field metaphor has really
worked (0.9) I think it kind of gets in people's
head an image. And images are very important in
change. Because the image that pops into
everybody's head (.) when they think of learning
is what?
(0.5)
Come on we all know. What's the first thing
which pops into everybody's head when they
think of lu- the word learning?
(0.2)
Audience: Schoolroo[m.

Senge: [Schoolroo:m. (0.5) Unfortunately schoolrooms have little to do with learning. (0.8) Right? This is a schoolroom. (0.7) One expe:rt you know a bunch of novices,=expert transmits,=novices receive:.=Novices then can .h if they have to be tested right? .hh Prove to the expert that they (.) received well. (0.8) And we call that learning? (0.5) It's not learning. (0.2) That's information transmission. (0.8) Machines do that by the way .h interestingly much better than human beings. .h Should be a clue?
(0.4)

Audience: L-L-L[LLLLLLL

Senge: [Right.=I mean (.) human beings are not pretty good- very good at information transmission. .hh Human beings are extraordinarily good at learning though.

Senge asks the audience members to identify "the image that pops into everybody's head when they think of . . . the word learning" (lines 4–6). (Note that the question presupposes that the answer should be obvious as it applies to everybody.) In the light of an absence of immediate response from the audience (line 7), Senge cajoles the audience members ("Come on we all know") and then reissues the question (lines 8–10). Subsequently, a member of the audience calls out an answer ("Schoolroom") which Senge accepts, (line 13) before proceeding to criticise this image of learning (lines 13–23). In cases like this then, Senge implicates audience members in the description of a state of affairs on which he subsequently expresses a view.

When Senge asks questions that invite audience members to respond by raising their hands (or declining to raise their hands, as the case may be), Senge uses either a two-part or three-part structure:

1 → He asks a question which establishes that most, if not all,

audience members belong to a particular group, a group to which Senge also belongs.

2 → He asks a question (real or rhetorical) based on this group membership, the answer to which carries the key message.

3 → In some cases, he goes on to explicitly state the key message.

In asking the questions, Senge leaves the audience in no doubt as to how he is expecting them to respond; he raises *his* hand and does so just before or immediately after the completions of his questions. Consider the following example in which Senge uses this technique to illustrate the generalizability of a problem faced by an Organisational Learning Group – namely that progress made at team level does not permeate through the wider organization due to the latter's hierarchical and bureaucratic structures.

**Extract 3.3 – "Extraordinary teams" [CTK: 0:10.15]**

Senge: What we experienced again and again we've experienced now and I'm saying we in this statement is those of us working together in the OLC Organisational Learning Consortium. (.) We've experienced extraordinary teams making extraordinary progress and then bumping up against (.) larger hierarchical bureaucratic institutions. (.) How many of you have ever been part of an extraordinary team in a larger bureaucratic [hierarchical institution?
[*Senge raises his hand*

Audience: *Audience members raise their hands (light laughter)*

Senge: Great. I mean keep your hands- well let me ask you a simple question for those of you who just raised your hands. How many of you have ever seen significant innovations that occurred in that team, what you have considered as

genuine demonstrated improvements in results (.) significant innovation (.) not spread to the larger [organization?
[*Senge raises his hand*

Audience: *Audience members raise their hands*

Senge: Okay. That is a core issue around quote organizational learning, Why do good ideas not spread? In fact many of us have come to the conclusion that actually modest improvements can spread very quickly. Real breakthroughs are extraordinarily difficult to spread in the larger organization.

Having asserted that significant breakthroughs at a team level are prevented from spreading through organizations due to hierarchical bureaucratic structures, Senge seeks to substantiate his point by eliciting a show of hands from (1) people who have been involved in teams that have achieved significant developments and (2) those among this self-identified group who have experienced the very problem he has identified. He then goes on to underline the message he is seeking to convey.

Interestingly, although these forms of speaker/audience interaction are not used by the other management gurus examined in this book, they do feature in the presentations of other gurus, in particular those given by Steven Covey.

### *Gary Hamel*

Gary Hamel adopts a quick-fire style that is not dissimilar to that of Tom Peters. However, like Peter Senge, he makes less use of colloquialisms and profanities. More importantly, he interacts with his audiences to a far lesser extent than do either Peters or Senge. For example, in contrast to Peters and Senge, Hamel stands towards the back of the stage and he tends to plough on with his lecture regardless of immediate audience reactions, whether individual or collective, to what he is saying. This is exemplified by the fact that, as we shall see in Chapter 4, when he evokes collective laughter from audience members he often talks across the laughter and thereby perhaps suppresses it (see Extract 4.5 on page 76). Consider the following example, which we shall revisit in subsequent chapters, in which Hamel praises the achievements of the coffee-shop chain, Starbucks, that has, he argues, adopted the practices he is recommending by elevating coffee into a highly desired product.

**Extract 3.4 – "Latte at Starbucks" [LinL: 0:38:30]**

Hamel: Let me give you some very (.) mundane
examples for a moment. (0.4) take something
that certainly in the United States we all know as
a a company Starbucks.=Now beginning to go
interna:tional. (0.7) Who would have predicted
here that you could get construction workers to
line up three deep to pay two and a half bucks
for a latte after all.

Audience: L[L L L L[L L L L L L L L L

Hamel: [Right. [And if- and if I'm sitting there inside
Nestlé running you know the world's largest
coffee brand Nescafe (0.5) how do I feel when in
less than ten years somebody can build a coffee
brand (0.6) that in the largest mar:ket er: coffee
drinking market in the world is a demonstrably
more valuable bra::nd (0.5) than my decades old
coffee brand.

Hamel's rhetorical question in lines 5–8 illustrates the success of Starbucks by describing how construction workers queue to buy lattes from their outlets and depicting this as an extraordinary and unforeseen achievement ("Who would have predicted . . ."). Having evoked collective audience laughter (line 9), Hamel reverts to a serious stance as he refers to the implications of Starbucks' success in the 'coffee business' for its competitor Nestlé on their well-established Nescafe brand. Notice, however, that he does not wait for the audience's laughter to subside before so doing (something, as we shall see, other gurus routinely do). Instead, he reconfirms his point ("Right") in overlap with the onset of laughter, and then moves on to discuss the case of Nestlé. This is typical of Hamel's style, which demonstrates little attention to the audience's reactions and involves very little interaction with the audience. As Morgan (2001: 116) observes, while Hamel is clearly a highly accomplished speaker in other respects, he 'simply offers (his audiences) the opportunity to listen to what he has to say'.

### *Rosabeth Moss Kanter*

Rosabeth Moss Kanter adopts a more distant and elevated style of speaking than Peters, avoiding profanity and making less use of colloquialisms and hyperbole. Although she interacts with her audience, this often comes across as less natural and stilted than in the case with either Peters or Senge. Nonetheless, as the following example indicates, she is far more responsive to the actions and reactions of audience members than is Hamel. In this extract, Kanter ridicules the attitude towards success that she suggests is prevalent in most American corporations.

**Extract 3.5 – "What success really means" [MC: 0.00.41]**

Kanter: D'you know what success <u>re</u>ally means in most American corporations, (0.4) well I mean money power prestige maybe,=and these things are <u>n</u>ice of course. (.) But what I <u>real</u>ly think success means (.) is it means never again (.) having to listen to anybody who disagrees with you.
(.) *RMK smiles slightly as she tilts her head to one side*

Audience: LLL[LLLLLLL LLLLLLL
[*Kanter's smile broadens*]

In this example, Kanter evokes laughter from the audience. In contrast to Hamel (see Extract 3.4 above), however, she clearly tailors her actions to take account of the audience member's response. Specifically, she not only cedes the floor to the audience after they begin to laugh but also broadens her smile. In other words, she *interacts* with her audience. More generally Kanter's style seeks to engage the audience and raise their attentiveness. A central feature of her talks are a number of extended stories (see Chapter 6), some of which she has told over a 10-year period, that she tells in an authoritative tone using a narrow range of volume and pitch.

In summary, this review shows that the gurus' styles of speaking differ from each other in several respects and that Peters' style cannot be regarded as a template for all gurus. Interestingly, when we have shown extracts from the gurus' lectures to postgraduate management students, it is these stylistic differences that initially attract their attention. It is only when we encourage the students to look more closely at the gurus' performances that the students recognize that these stylistic differences are underpinned by the use of a common set of speaking practices concerning (1) the management of criticism and (2) the verbal structuring of messages.

## Managing criticism

Often, the gurus extol the virtues of practices that the audience members are unlikely to be using and/or criticize practices that they are likely to be using. However, the gurus are careful to avoid directly criticizing their audiences. When they praise organizational practices, they do not draw attention to the fact that the audience members may not be using them. And when they criticize management practices, with rare exceptions (which are heavily mitigated), they do not direct their criticism at the audience members who are using them. Instead, they direct their disparagement at third-party organizations and managers, who are often unnamed. Consider the following example in which Gary Hamel is bemoaning the 'fact' that American organizations have taken a reactive rather than a proactive approach to strategic planning. Hamel uses American automobile companies as an example, arguing that for 30 years they have been content to follow the lead of the Japanese.

**Extract 3.6 – "Call Toyota" [LinL: 0:00:00]**

| | |
|---|---|
| Hamel: | because it's no longer enough simply to worry about is my organization fit.=The question is (.) who is setting the transformation agenda in your industry today. (0.7) For the last thirty years the transformation agenda for the American automobile industry was set by Toyota and Honda. =That is not a good way to live. (0.8) er You know the (.) Japanese started working on lean manufacturing we said that's important.=they redesigned the supplier network,=oh maybe we should do that.-They worked on quality.=Oh that seems to be important too. (0.8) In fact I one time was sitting with the head of strategic planning for one of America's er largest automobile companies, (0.6) I said frankly I don't know why your company needs you. (0.4) It seems pretty simple.=When your company's done doing one thing why don't they just pick up the phone, call Toyota and ask them what's next..=Right.=I mean |
| Audience: | LLL[LLL |
| Hamel: | [how hard is that. (0.6) So this- this I think is the new competitive agenda. (0.7) |

Hamel mounts a scathing attack on American automobile companies and an unnamed executive as he makes the case for American companies in general adopting a new approach to strategic planning. It is highly likely that many, if not all, of the members of his audience will not be using this approach at the present time. Indeed, if they were doing so, it would be nonsensical for Gary Hamel to be lecturing to them on this topic. However, Hamel does not directly confront his audience by drawing attention to the likelihood that they are guilty of the same sins as the automobile companies and executive that he refers to.

In the following extract Peters adopts a similar practice during the telling of a humorous story about his experiences of trying to go shopping in a local store on Christmas Eve. This comes at the end of his lecture and is intended to illustrate, through a contrary example, many of the points he has been making on what 'service with soul' means. While humorous, the story is critical. Indeed, in lines 10–12 he says that he will refrain from revealing the identity of the store because he feels so strongly about their poor level of service he may end up 'uttering a whole string of obscenities'.

**Extract 3.7 – 'Visit to grocery store' [SwS: 1.06.54]**

Peters: I want to relate one (.) one other little story because again this brings home so much the essence of it doesn't take an electron microscope and the notion of (.) of you know the (.) the (.) the soul issue (0.4) S.O.U.L in customer satisfaction, love, affection, (0.2) whatever sets of words. (0.5) I think it was like Christmas Eve last year, (.) I had to do, (0.2) almost all of us have to do some last minute shopping OK. And: I go down to our local chain store, (.) which I will not mention by name because I can't do so without uttering a whole string of obscenities.

Audience: LL[LLLL-L-L-L

Peters: [So (.) I go into this store.

When the gurus anonymize their targets they may be adhering to the common consultancy practice of respecting the confidentiality of clients. But such an approach also enables the gurus to manage potential criticism as the audience is not presented with a target for which they can have positive or negative feelings. Furthermore, without knowing the identity of the manager or organization being discussed there is no way in which audience members can independently assess and so challenge what the guru is saying. Whatever the reasons for this approach, it enables the gurus to question common management practices without directly confronting the audience members who may be using them. In this way the gurus lessen the possibility that their comments may alienate or offend a section of the audience and so receive a negative response such as booing or heckling.

## Verbal structuring of messages

As noted above, a number of studies explain the gurus' oratorical power in terms of their use of the rhetorical devices identified in the seminal work of Atkinson (1984a, 1984b) on political oratory (see also Heritage and Greatbatch, 1986). These authors identify seven devices that, when they are used effectively, fortify, highlight and project speakers' messages (making them more memorable). Critically, they are also often associated with the elicitation of applause during political speeches:

(1) *Contrasts.* Contrasts comprise two juxtapositioned sentences (A→, B→) that are opposed in words, or sense, or both and in the process emphasize messages by making the core assertion twice – in a 'positive' and 'negative' form:

**Extract 3.8 – [Conservative Party Conference 1999]**

| | |
|---|---|
| Hague: | And it was in the nineteen eighties (.) that |
| A → | it was the forces of conservatism (.) that stood up to the unions<br>And defended our country<br>(.) |
| B → | while Tony Blair was voting against every trade |

| | |
|---|---|
| | union law and campaigning [for unilateral disarmament. |
| Audience: | Applause (8.5 seconds) |

(2) *Lists, especially those including three items (1→, 2→, 3→).* The repetition of an item can serve, as Atkinson (1984b: 60) puts it, 'to strengthen, underline and amplify almost any kind of message'. This is sometimes done by producing a list that contains three identical items. For example, 'education, education, education', the rallying cry of the British Labour Party during the 1997 general election. More usually, however, three-part lists in political contexts involve more than repeating the same words, as in the following example:

**Extract 3.9 – [Liberal Democrat Party Conference 1999]**

| | |
|---|---|
| Kennedy: | But they should be even more ashamed of something else. (.) When they start as- supposedly progressive government starts using the language of the need for a moral crusade. |
| 1 → | There's more to morality than curfews Mister Straw. |
| | (.) |
| 2 → | There's more to morality than a tax on people (.) who choose to bring up their children in their own way. |
| | (.) |
| 3 → | And there's a lot more to morality (.) than some of the most illiberal asylum and immigration laws that this country has ever seen. |
| Audience: | Applause (7.8 seconds) |

(3) *Puzzle–solution formats*. Puzzle–solutions involve speakers establishing a puzzle (P—>) in the minds of audience members before offering as a solution (S—>) to the puzzle a statement that embodies the core message they wish to get across. The core message is emphasized by the puzzle, which invites the audience to anticipate or guess the solution and, by the same token, listen to the speaker's own solution when it is delivered. This is illustrated in the next extract.

**Extract 3.10 – [Labour Party Conference 1999]**

| | | |
|---|---|---|
| Blair: | P—> | And here's one for us to put back down the Tory throats |
| | | (.) |
| | S—> | fewer days lost in strikes than in any of the eighteen years of Tory government. |
| Audience: | | Applause |

(4) *Headline–punchline*. Headline–punchlines are structurally similar to the puzzle–solution format described above. Here the speaker indicates that they are about to make a declaration, pledge or announcement (H—>) and then proceeds to make it (P—>). The message is emphasized by the speaker's announcement in advance of what he or she is about to say. This format is illustrated in the following example.

**Extract 3.11 – [Heritage and Greatbatch, 1986: 129]**

| | | |
|---|---|---|
| Meadowcroft: | | The other point about that as we:ll (.) and this is very very important I think, (0.3) is that passing this motion (.) can help the Alliance with the Social Democrats. |
| | | (.) |
| | H—> | and I'll tell you why:. |

| | |
|---|---|
| | (.) |
| P—> | It remo:ves the last excuse for your idealistic radicals to join the Labour Party. |
| Audience: | Applause (8.0 seconds) |

(5) *Combinations.* All of the devices outlined above may be combined with one another with the result that the message will be still further emphasized. As the example below shows, the most common combination is a contrast together with another device, in this case a puzzle–solution.

**Extract 3.12 – [Heritage and Greatbatch, 1986: 130–131]**

(In this case a puzzle (P—>) is resolved (S—>) by a contrast (a—> b—>))

| | |
|---|---|
| Jones: P—> | You know Mister Chairman er Margaret Thatcher and Ted Heath (0.4) both have great vision. |
| | (0.7) |
| S—> a—> | The difference i:s that Margaret Thatcher (0.20 has a vision that one day Britain will be great agai:n |
| | (0.4) |
| b—> | and Ted Heath has a vision (0.2) that one day Ted Heath will be great again.= |
| Audience: | Applause (19.4 seconds) |

(6) *Position taking.* Position taking (PT—>) involves a speaker first describing a state of affairs and then overtly and unequivocally praising or condemning the state of affairs described. The

description involves little or no overt evaluation. An example of simple position taking is illustrated below.

**Extract 3.13 – [Heritage and Greatbatch, 1986: 131]**

Batiste: There is a widespread practice in this country (.) whereby companies which use closed shops (.) pass that obligation on to small business sub-contractors (.) to use only s- sh- er- er union labour (.) in meeting contracts in those places.
(.)
PT → That practice must stop.

Audience: Applause (6.2 seconds)

(7) *Pursuits.* Pursuits (→) involve speakers recompleting or resummarizing a previous point. As the extract below shows it inevitably involves reemphasizing the original point.

**Extract 3.14 – [Heritage and Greatbatch, 1986: 134]**

(In this case the pursuit follows a three-part list which fails to evoke applause)

Evans: And you come to selling
(0.2)
1 → We've got to sell Great Britain
(0.2)
2 → We've got to sell Margaret Thatcher
(0.2)
3 → We've got to sell her policies (.) to the people
(.)
Pursuit → Tell the people [(0.2) what the pla:n is.

Audience: Applause (8.7 seconds)

These rhetorical devices were all well-known to ancient Greek scholars of rhetoric. The use of contrasts (antithesis), for example, was first taught by the Sophists such as Corax, Tisias and Gorgias from the fifth century BC (Dobson, 1919) and was deeply engrained in the Greek mentality by the constant use of the grammatical construction 'on the one hand, . . . but on the other . . .', and from their fondness for contrasting figures like Prometheus and Epimetheus (Kennedy, 1963, 1994). Atkinson and his followers show that these techniques are very much alive and well today. In addition to identifying how the devices are actually used in speeches to invite, and to provide for the coordination of, applause, they show that they have a broader significance, arguing that they are central to *all* forms of persuasive speaking and writing. They are a key means through which speakers and writers emphasize messages and make them stand out.

A review of the gurus' lectures reveals that they are replete with examples of these rhetorical techniques. As we show in the next chapter, the use of the devices is associated with the elicitation of audience responses, predominantly laughter. However, the gurus use them throughout their lectures, regardless of whether they are seeking to evoke collective responses from audience members. Despite the variations in their styles of speaking discussed above, all the gurus use these devices to package their core messages. In so doing, they draw largely on three of the devices – contrasts, lists and puzzle–solutions, which they often use in combination with one another at key moments in their lectures.

Consider the following example, which was identified by members of the Tom Peters Group as the speech segment that had the most impact on delegates at their training sessions, during which extracts from video recordings of Peters' lectures are played. The segment follows a case study during which Peters has related his experiences while visiting a sausage-making company that offers professional and personal development opportunities to all of its employees. Following the story, Peters explicitly identifies the lessons that are to be learnt from the things he observed at the company's premises. In so doing, Peters characteristically uses colloquial language (e.g. "rip you off"), profanities ("get the hell out . . ."), hyperbole (30 or 40 nano-seconds) and metaphor ("fly to the moon without a face mask"). However, his core message(s) concerning the lessons to be drawn from one of his case studies is packaged in an elegant combination of puzzle–solution formats (P→, S→), a contrast (A→, B→) and three-part lists (1→, 2→, 3→).

**Extract 3.15 – 'What do you see?' [TPE2: 0.23.30]**

Peters: P → There's a lot of stuff that's important here,
S/4pl → teams,= training compensation(.) pay for
knowledge,=profit sharing, =stock owner-
ship,
Pursuit → =there are a hundred variables that are
involved.
(.)
P → But the whole thing in my mind can be
literally boiled down to one question. (.) And
it is a question which managing directors and
factory managers and accounting managers
and MIS managers have got to ask them-
selves.
(.)
S → P → And the one simple question (.) which is the
most profound question affecting Great
Britain and the United States of America's
economic future (.) is what do you and your
colleagues as managers see (.) really see (.)
when you look in the eye of a first-line
employee.
(.)
S → A → Do you see a ne'er do well
(.)
1 → who needs that span of control of 1 to 6
which is present in your company?
2 → Who would rip you off if you turned your
back for more that 30 or 40 nanoseconds.
(.)

3 → Who requires a five hundred-page policy manual which tells you when to go to the bathroom.
(.)
B→ Or do you see a person (.) who could literally fly to the moon without a face mask if only you
1 → would train the hell out of them,
2 → get the hell out of their way,
3 → and give them something worth doing.

Peters begins by establishing a puzzle in the minds of his audience, *viz* what does he, Peters, think is important? He then provides a solution, which is formatted as a four-part list (lines 2–4), followed by a 'pursuit' (lines 5–6). Subsequently, Peters establishes a second puzzle – what is it that "managers have got to ask themselves" (lines 8–13), the solution to which establishes yet another puzzle (lines 15–21), namely what do managers see when they "look in the eye of a first-line employee". The solution to this third and final puzzle carries the core message that Peters wishes to get across to the members of his audience. This is formulated as a contrast, which juxtapositions a negative managerial view of employees (lines 23–32) with a positive managerial view (lines 34–39). Each part of the contrast is formulated as a three-part list.

In the following extract, Kanter characteristically adopts a more restrained 'academic' approach than does Peters, as she ends her lecture on managing change. However, she deploys an equally impressive combination of finely crafted rhetorical devices as she delivers her key messages.

**Extract 3.16 – "Success takes time' [MC: 0:22.35]**

Kanter: People aren't necessarily just threatened by ideas'=it's when it becomes a reality and it

| | |
|---|---|
| | looks like now it's going to affect my job |
| P-> | because remember another important truth |
| | about innovation. |
| S-> A-> | And that is that it is my innovation |
| B-> | Is your headache. |
| | (.) |
| P-> | And there's another lesson that a friend of |
| | mine in Silicon Valley is fond of reminding |
| | people who have looked for fast results and |
| | expect changes to happen over night. |
| | (.) |
| S-> | He's fond of telling them that instant success |
| | takes time. |
| Audience: | LLLL |
| Kanter: A-> | Those things that suddenly spring up looking |
| | (.) as though they happened over night |
| | (.) |
| B-> | really are the results of an immense amount |
| | of team work (.) |
| | flexibility (.) and planning and replanning that |
| | allow people to persist (.) even when top |
| | management is losing faith (.) in order to |
| | make a valuable new idea come into being. I |
| | think |
| A-> 3pl-> | these skills, these lessons (.) these learnings |
| | can produce masters |
| B-> | not victims of change. |
| A-> 3pl-> | That is people who are producing and antici- |
| | pating and leading the changes |
| B-> | rather than simply reacting to somebody |
| | else's. |
| | Thank you. And enjoy the conference. |
| Audience: | xxxxx |

This passage begins with two puzzle–solutions (line 4–5 and lines 9–12), the solution to the first of which is formatted as a contrast. After the audience laughter (line 16), which was evoked by the second puzzle–solution format, dies away, Kanter produces three successive contrasts (lines 17–26, lines 27–29, and lines 30–34). The first components of the second and third of these contrasts are formatted as three-part lists (lines 27–28 and lines 30–31).

We could just as easily have used examples from Hamel and Senge to illustrate the pervasiveness of contrasts, lists and puzzle–solution formats. All the gurus exhibit an ability to use these devices to good effect, which is to say in well-balanced, readily understandable ways. Perhaps most importantly, at key junctures in their lectures they all routinely opt to maximize the impact of their messages by using the devices in combination with one another. Although it is not possible to establish whether the gurus succeeded in persuading their audiences to accept their ideas and visions, their skilful use of the devices is likely to have contributed to the memorability of what they said. At the very least, it is likely that their messages lingered in the minds of audience members, regardless of whether or not they agreed with them.

## Conclusion

The gurus do not adhere to a single style of speaking. They use colloquialisms, hyperbole, variations in intonation and pitch and the like to different degrees, and interact (or not) with members of their audiences in different ways. However, the gurus draw on the same ensemble of presentational techniques in order to deflect criticism away from audience members despite advocating practices that the audience members are unlikely to be using and/or criticizing practices that audience members are likely to be using. The ability of gurus to do this may be critical to understanding their success on the international management lecture circuit because, while managers may welcome exposure to ideas that question what they do, most will not wish to place themselves in situations in which they will be directly confronted.

The gurus also use the same techniques to highlight their core messages. Specifically, they routinely use the rhetorical devices discussed by Atkinson in his studies of political oratory. However, while these devices – contrasts, lists, puzzle–solutions, etc. – undoubtedly play a major role in the gurus' lectures, it does not follow, as previous studies of management gurus' oratory have suggested, that the effective use of these devices is *the* key to understanding the gurus' success on the management lecture circuit. As we demonstrate in remainder of this book, the gurus use a range of verbal and non-verbal techniques, some of which are arguably just as important as contrasts, three-part lists and the like.

Chapter 4

# Generating collective audience response

We have previously argued that a successful management guru needs to be an outstandingly effective public orator to establish and retain a prominent position on the international management lecture circuit. Their public performances provide opportunities to communicate their ideas to diverse audiences and in the process build their personal reputations and generate a very healthy income. When delivering a public speech gurus have to be sensitive to the needs of the audience and communicate their messages in such a way that they receive a positive response, otherwise their reputation as a public speaker will diminish. They therefore have to stir their audiences in some way. They achieve this since during their speeches the audience do not sit mute maintaining respectful silence. These are not episodes of one-way communication in which the speaker sends a message and the audience passively receive it. Rather the members of the audience actively participate in the proceedings. Indeed, their reactions are both shaped by and shape the emerging speech and therefore influence its unfolding interpretation. Unlike the example of Tony Blair's speech to the Women's Institute mentioned at the start of the book, these are not events characterized by demonstrations of disaffiliation. They do not contain any disaffiliative responses such as booing and heckling. Rather the audience members regularly produce displays of affiliation with the gurus by, *inter alia*, clapping, laughing supportively, nodding their heads and smiling. In some cases, these affiliative responses are produced by one or two individuals. In others, however, they involve numerous audience members acting in concert with each other.

Our analysis of the video recordings of the gurus' lectures indicates that when audience members collectively display their affiliation with the gurus', they do so predominantly by laughing in response to purportedly humorous messages. In this chapter, we demonstrate that collective audience laughter is not simply a spontaneous reaction to messages whose content is self-evidently humorous, but rather is 'invited' by the gurus through the use of a range of verbal and non-verbal practices. Mastery of these practices is critical because, as we show in Chapter 5, the elicitation of audience laughter plays an important role with regards to the expression of group cohesion and solidarity during the gurus' lectures and, when used effectively, it heightens audience attentiveness and makes the gurus' messages more memorable. Before discussing the practices, however, a brief review of the prior conversation analytic (CA) research on the generation of collective audience responses in public speaking contexts is necessary.

## Previous CA research on the generation of audience response

During the last 25 years a steady stream of CA studies of public speaking have examined the interactional practices through which speakers and audience members produce, interpret and co-ordinate their actions. The great majority of these studies have focussed on the elicitation and co-ordination of collective audience responses, such as applause and laughter, during political meetings. In so doing, they have demonstrated that such responses are not simply spontaneous reactions to the messages that evoke them (e.g. Atkinson, 1984a, 1984b; Clayman, 1992, 1993; Heritage and Greatbatch, 1986). As collective actions, their production is underpinned by the basic sociological principle that people prefer to act like those around them so as to avoid social isolation (Asch, 1951). Thus, for example, while individual audience members may wish to clap or laugh in response to public speakers' remarks, they will generally only do so in situations in which they are assured that other audience members will do the same. If this is not the case they may be found to be isolated in indicating their response to the speaker's foregoing remarks and socially embarrassed as a consequence. Thus a key issue for audience members is to gauge when and how to respond appropriately.

According to Clayman (1993: 111–113) collective responses may be facilitated by two methods – independent decision-making and mutual monitoring. Independent decision-making involves audience members reacting independently of one another, but nonetheless managing to respond in concert. In this respect, audience members gravitate to those parts of the speech that stand out conspicuously from other parts of the talk. Where audience members can anticipate the completion of such a message then 'its completion may serve as a common reference point around which individual response decisions are coordinated' (Clayman, 1993: 112). In contrast, mutual monitoring involves individual response decisions being 'guided, at least in part, by reference to the [aural or, less commonly, visual] behaviour of other audience members' (Clayman, 1993: 112). Thus, for example, individual audience members may decide to respond after they observe others either doing likewise or acting in ways that suggest that they are about to do so (e.g. preparing to clap, murmuring approval, and nodding). As Clayman observes, these two scenarios lead to different types of responses:

> Responses organized primarily by independent decision-making should begin with a 'burst' that quickly builds to maximum intensity as many audience members begin to respond in concert. Mutual monitoring, by contrast, should result in a 'staggered' onset as the initial reactions of a few audience members prompt others to respond. These scenarios are not mutually exclusive – a response episode may begin with a 'burst' involving many independent starters, which subsequently encourages others to join in, Indeed, an initial 'burst' should be most effective in prompting others because it *decisively* establishes the relevance of a response and *decisively* counteracts concerns about isolation.
>
> (Clayman, 1993: 112)

Conversation analytic studies of political oratory demonstrate that the onset of applause is organized primarily by independent decision-making (Atkinson, 1984a, 1984b). Generally, applause begins with a 'burst' immediately after or just before the completion of a focal message, reaches its maximum intensity after the first second or so, remains more or less constant for a further five seconds and then falls away. Applause episodes are rarely more than 8 seconds in duration. Heritage and Greatbatch (1986: 112) report that most applause is initiated within 0.3 seconds and the opportunity to applaud is lost after 0.5 seconds. Thus each audience member must arrive at a decision whether to applaud in a very short space of time and in a context in which the value of such an action may rely on the independent decisions of perhaps many hundreds of others. Individual audience members are able to respond in concert because political speakers indicate clearly to them when applause is relevant. Atkinson shows that political speakers often accomplish this not only by (1) using prosodic, rhythmic and non-vocal signals to mark out messages from a background of other speech material, but also by (2) packaging their messages in a small number of rhetorical devices which both emphasize them and provide them with clearly projectable message completion points around which individual audience members can anticipate and co-ordinate their actions. The latter devices are those that we discussed in Chapter 3: contrasts, lists, puzzle–solutions, headline–punchlines, combinations, position-taking, and pursuits. Atkinson and his associates show how these devices are used in speeches to invite, and to provide for the coordination of, applause. As such, they are a vital part of the way effective speakers convey their messages and can be heard whenever someone is trying to elicit a positive audience response. They are an essential element of persuasive oratory. A more detailed description of all seven devices can be found in Heritage and Greatbatch (1986: 122–137), whose analysis of political speeches delivered to the British Conservative, Labour and Liberal party conferences in 1981 revealed that just over two-thirds of the instances of full-scale applause in the speeches occurred in response to messages that were packaged in one or more of the rhetorical formats.

Several researchers have developed Atkinson's work by examining not only applause (e.g. Brodine, 1986; Bull, 1986; Grady and

Potter, 1985; Heritage and Greatbatch, 1986) but also audience laughter (Clayman, 1992) and booing and heckling (e.g. Clayman, 1993; McIlvenny, 1996). What this latter research shows is that incipiently disaffiliative responses are generally organized differently to applause. Booing, for example, begins some time after the completion of the objectionable item. It is not triggered solely by the speaker. Rather booing is often preceded by some other form of audience response, such as clapping, shouting or a buzz in the audience. Thus, when audience members boo they tend to wait until other audience behaviours have been initiated. These reactions may follow the delivery of a message in a timely fashion and in the process delay the booing as the audience members monitor each other's conduct. As Clayman (1993: 117) points out, in intervening, these 'triggers' give time for mutual monitoring to occur and so facilitate the co-ordination of booing within the audience.

In summary, research into affiliative and disaffiliative audience responses shows that agreements tend to be produced promptly whereas disagreements are typically delayed. They are thus positioned differently *vis-à-vis* the remarks they are responding to. Since applause is usually expressed without delay it is co-ordinated through independent decision-making. In contrast, given that booing is delayed, this time lag allows mutual monitoring to guide the onset of the response.

While this research reveals the interactional organization of a range of speaker–audience conduct it has focused exclusively on various forms of political oratory, with the result that relatively little is known about whether and how the verbal and non-verbal practices deployed by political speakers are used in other types of public speaking. However, as we have seen, Atkinson (1984a, 1984b) suggests that these devices are not restricted to political oratory or the elicitation of applause but have a powerful appeal when used effectively in a wide range of contexts where the aim is to persuade an audience. We pursue this point in the remainder of the chapter by examining the techniques used by management gurus, another group of speakers whose initial and continuing success depends to a large extent on their ability to build personal reputations as powerful orators.

## How management gurus invite audience laughter

The distribution of audience response in the gurus' lectures is summarized in Table 4.1 overleaf. This shows that the lectures contain ninety-nine cases of collective audience laughter, whereas applause is confined to the beginning and end of the gurus' presentations and to three incidents during Tom Peters's lectures where laughter leads to applause, one of which involves only a handful of people clapping.[1] In this respect, the gurus' lectures are akin to various forms of public speaking, including university lectures and training seminars, in which applause is usually not treated as a relevant activity either on its own or in conjunction with laughter.

In this section we first examine how the gurus invite audience laughter by projecting clear message completion points and signalling their humorous intent. We then discuss how the gurus subsequently confirm/disconfirm the relevance of laughter.

### *Projecting message completion points*

Earlier in this chapter we noted that collective audience responses may be facilitated by two methods: independent decision-making (which involves audience members independently recognizing that and when some form of response is relevant) and mutual monitoring (which involves audience members reacting to the aural and visual actions of a few of their counterparts). Responses that are mainly facilitated by independent decision-making begin with a 'burst' and quickly grow in intensity as numerous audience members respond in concert. Responses that are primarily organized by mutual monitoring are characterized by 'staggered' onsets as the reactions of a handful of audience members encourage others to respond in the same fashion.

In the case of the gurus' lectures, independent decision-making plays a predominant role in the genesis of audience laughter. Thus, as Table 4.2 shows, 93 (92%) cases of laughter begin with a burst, either just before or immediately after message completion. As our earlier review of research on political oratory indicated, the ability of individual audience members to respond in concert at or near to message completion points depends upon speakers supplying their messages with emphasis and clearly projectable completion points

*Table 4.1* Incidence of audience laughter in the gurus' lectures

| | *TP* | *RMK* | *PS* | *GH* | *Total* |
|---|---|---|---|---|---|
| Full laughter | 43 | 25 | 20 | 11 | 99 |

Note
TP, Tom Peters; RMK, Rosabeth Moss Kanter; PS, Peter Senge; GH, Gary Hamel.

*Table 4.2* Immediate bursts of laughter and laughter whose onset is staggered

| | *TP* | *RK* | *PS* | *GH* | *Totals* |
|---|---|---|---|---|---|
| Immediate bursts | 42 | 24 | 17 | 10 | 93 |
| Staggered onsets | 1 | 1 | 3 | 1 | 6 |
| Totals | 43 | 25 | 20 | 11 | 99 |

Note
TP, Tom Peters; RMK, Rosabeth Moss Kanter; PS, Peter Senge; GH, Gary Hamel.

around which audience members can co-ordinate their actions. In just under half (46) of the cases of collective laughter the gurus achieve this by using one or more of the seven rhetorical formats associated with the generation of applause at political meetings. Consider Extract 4.1 in which Tom Peters supports his argument that organizations should adopt 'flat and fluid' structures by quoting Ross Perot. The quotation praises one company, Electronic Data Systems (EDS) for purportedly adopting a 'flat and fluid' structure, and disparages another company, General Motors (GM), for purportedly retaining a cumbersome bureaucratic structure. Both the commendation of EDS and the criticism of GM are followed by audience laughter.

**Extract 4.1 – "When you see a snake" [TOC2: 35.56]**

| | | |
|---|---|---|
| 1 | Peters: | My favourite <u>Perro</u>ism of all was his |
| 2 | | description, <u>right</u> before leaving GM, of |

what he sa:w as the difference between
Electronic Data Systems and GM. (0.6)
He said,
["At EDS (.) WHEN YOU SEE A SNAKE
[*Leans forward, glares, uses angry tone of*
*voice*
(.) YOU KILL IT".

Audience: → [LLLLLLLLL LLLLLLLLL LLLLL-L-L[-L
[*Turns and walks* ]

Peters: [He said, "At GM when you see a snake,
[you search the world for the top
[*Leans forward/smile face*
consultant on snakes.

Audience: → LLLLLLLLL LLLLLLLLL

Peters: Then you appoint a committee on snakes
and you study snakes for the next two
years. (1.0) <Flat (.) fluid (.) and get on
with it (.) that':s the creature.

Peters provides the messages that evoke laughter with both emphasis and clearly projectable completion points by, *inter alia*, using a puzzle–solution format (similar to the example in Chapter 3). Thus he begins by establishing a puzzle in the minds of the audience members (lines 1–4): what did Ross Perot see as the difference between EDS and GM? He then offers a two-part solution which is formed as a contrast (lines 6–9 and 12–15). In this way, he highlights the contents of the messages against a background of surrounding speech materials. He also provides the audience members with resources to anticipate the completion of the two messages, for they can match each part of the emerging solution to the puzzle in order to infer what it will take for it to be complete. In the case of the second part of the solution/contrast, they can also match it against the first part. In both instances, Peters confirms the relevance of laughter by ceding the floor until the audience's laughter ends and then, when he resumes speaking, neither asserting nor otherwise indicating that the audience's laughter was inappropriate or unexpected (lines 13–15).

In the 47 cases in which the gurus do not use the verbal devices discussed by Atkinson, the gurus nonetheless supply messages which precipitate laughter with emphasis and clearly projectable completion points. Consider Extract 4.2 in which audience laughter occurs after Rosabeth Moss Kanter derides a product name, 'Zoo Doo' (although she adopts a positive stance in relation to the product per se).

**Extract 4.2 – "Zoo Doo" [MC: 00.06.19]**

Kanter: Now if it had been in New England (.) that
person would ne(h)ver ha(h)d dar(h)ed speak
up, but because it was California they are:
(0.7) making their animals a profit centre.=Like
the Toronto Zoo by the way that has been
packaging fertiliser that they sell which has been
contributed by the animals at the Toronto Zoo.
(.) The Bronx Zoo also has one like this on the
market I hate to say this out loud in front of
several thousand people but they do have it on
the market (.) under the brand na:me (.)
[Zoo Doo.
[*RMK purses lips and widens eyes.*

Audience: LLLLLLLLL LL[LLL (1.5)

Kanter: [Well you'll see my point in a
minute, I'm no(h)t ju(h)st try(h)ing to entertain
you. (.) Because one more round of the
elephant,=I then thought . . . ((Continues))

Although Kanter does not use any of the rhetorical devices (e.g. a contrast, list, puzzle–solution format) discussed in CA research on political oratory, a large number of the audience members independently anticipate the completion of her message. This is due, in part, to the fact that she nonetheless both emphasizes her message and provides it with a clearly projectable completion point. On the one hand, she draws attention to her message, and thereby highlights it, by announcing that she is going to say something that is potentially 'delicate' or undesirable (lines 9–10: "I hate to say this in front of several thousand people . . ."). On the other hand, she provides her message with a clearly projectable completion point by (1) indicating that she is referring to a brand name and (2) using a syntactic structure which clearly indicates that the brand name will be revealed at the end of the sentence in progress (lines 10–11: "they do have it on the market under the brand na:me"). Consequently, as the sentence unfolds, the audience members are in a position to anticipate that message and sentence completion will coincide with Kanters' articulation of the brand name 'Zoo Doo'. Notice, moreover, that Kanter pauses just prior to producing the brand name (line 11: (.)), thereby providing the audience with a little extra time in which to gear up to respond (what Atkinson refers to as a monitor space). So, despite the absence of the rhetorical formats examined in research on political oratory, the same principles apply: the speaker both emphasizes her message and provides it with a clearly projectable completion point. Subsequently, Kanter confirms the relevance of laughter by, *inter alia*, remaining silent until the audiences' response starts to die away (lines 14–15).

In addition to providing messages that precipitate laughter with emphasis and clearly projectable completion points, the gurus also provide them with additional stress via a range of prosodic, rhythmic and non-vocal signals which mark out messages from a background of other speech material, and thereby indicate the relevance of audience response to them. In assessing the role of vocal and non-vocal cues in the generation of laughter, we used the scheme devised by Heritage and Greatbatch (1986) in their analysis of political speech-making. This involves coding each message which evoked laughter in terms of its degree of stress:

> Stress was evaluated by taking note of (1) whether the speaker was gazing at the audience at or near the completion of a

> message; whether the message was (2) delivered more loudly than surrounding speech passages, or (3) with greater pitch or stress variation, or (4) with marked speeding up, slowing down, or some other rhythmic shift, or (5) accompanied by the use of gestures. In the absence of any of these features, the message was coded 'no stress'. One of these features was treated as sufficient for an 'intermediate stress' coding, whereas the presence of two or more features resulted in a coding of 'full stress'.
>
> (Heritage and Greatbatch, 1986: 143)

As Table 4.3 shows, 74 messages had full stress (including those in Extracts 4.1 and 4.2 above), 21 had intermediate stress, while only 4 had no stress.

In summary, the 93 messages which precipitate immediate bursts of audience laughter: (1) have clearly projectable completion points around which audience members can co-ordinate their actions (regardless of whether they are packaged in the verbal devices identified in prior CA research on political oratory); and, (2) are nearly all stressed so that they stand out from surrounding speech materials. In these regards, they follow the same principles as messages that elicit applause. However, as we show in the next section, the gurus also routinely deploy additional techniques that are specifically associated with the generation of audience laughter.

*Table 4.3* Stress

| | *Full* | *Intermediate* | *None* | *Totals* |
|---|---|---|---|---|
| TP | 31 | 11 | 1 | 43 |
| RMK | 18 | 6 | 1 | 25 |
| PS | 17 | 2 | 1 | 20 |
| GH | 8 | 2 | 1 | 11 |
| Totals | 74 | 21 | 4 | 99 |

Note
TP, Tom Peters; RMK, Rosabeth Moss Kanter; PS, Peter Senge; GH, Gary Hamel.

## Establishing the relevance of laughter

The gurus rarely rely on audience members to recognize that collective laughter is relevant on the basis of the content of their messages alone. Rather, they also establish the relevance of audience laughter through the use of a range of verbal and non-verbal actions during the delivery, and/or following the completion, of their messages. These include: (1) announcing that they are about to say something humorous; (2) smiling or laughing; and/or (3) using 'comedic' facial expressions, gestures and prosody. The latter involve, for example, displays of disgust, disbelief, anger, horror, amazement or some other emotional reaction by themselves or others to the actions, practices or issues that are being discussed. This is not to say that these non-verbal actions are inherently 'comedic'. Their possible status as such derives from their use with particular verbal messages and devices, whose 'comedic' status in turn derives in part from their use with such non-verbal actions. In other words, the speakers' verbal and non-verbal actions are reflexively related – the comedic status of each resting in part on their use in conjunction with the other.

In 16 cases it was not possible to establish with certainty whether or not such cues had been used to signal humorous intent because the gurus' facial expressions and/or bodily actions were not visible (in the recordings) as they delivered their messages. However, as Table 4.4 shows, just under 80 per cent (62) of the remaining (78) cases involve the use by the gurus of 'comedic' cues during the delivery of their verbal messages.

*Table 4.4* The use of comedic cues in the context of messages that evoke immediate bursts of audience laughter

| | |
|---|---|
| Cues during delivery | 62 |
| Cues after delivery only | 6 |
| No cues | 9 |
| Don't know | 16 |
| Total | 94 |

Thus, for example, in Extract 4.1 on page 65 Tom Peters does not solely rely on the 'humourous' content of his remarks to establish the relevance of audience laughter; he also 'invites' audience laughter through the use of a range of non-verbal techniques. In the first case of laughter (line 10), which follows Peters's depiction of Perot's commendation of EDS, Peters uses comedic gestures, facial expressions and prosody. As he quotes Perot on EDS (lines 6–9), he suddenly leans forward, glares at a section of the audience and speaks louder as he adopts a 'mock angry' tone. Then, as he completes the quotation ("you kill it"), he bares his teeth as he 'spits' out the words. Together with Perot's incongruous metaphorical imagery – seeing and killing snakes in a corporate context – Peters's non-verbal actions establish the possible relevance of audience laughter. In the second case of audience laughter (line 16), which follows Peters's depiction of Perot's disparagement of GM (lines 12–15), Peters, reverting to a 'low key' form of speech delivery, establishes the possible relevance of laughter by leaning forward and smiling at the audience as he completes the quotation. Rosabeth Moss Kanter also uses non-verbal techniques to signal humorous intent in Extract 4.2 on page 67. As she utters the brand name 'Zoo Doo' her facial expression conveys her apparent distaste or discomfit at having to say the name out loud (lines 9–12) and, as she completes the sentence, she purses her lips and widens her eyes as she stares at the audience (line 13). Like Peters, then, Kanter does not solely rely on the content of her message to indicate to the audience members that her message is humorous and that laughter is an appropriate response.

In the remaining 15 cases the gurus deliver messages without using non-verbal cues which are, in the context of their other actions, recognizably 'comedic'. In these cases, then, those audience members who laugh just before or immediately after message completion appear to do so on the basis of the content of the gurus' messages alone. Consider Extract 4.3 in which Peter Senge concedes that a concept (infrastructure), which has been central to his theory about organizational learning, is inappropriate.

**Extract 4.3 – "Infrastructure" [FD: 0.48.50]**

(Discussing co-edited volume: *The Fifth Discipline Field Book*)

Senge: So what infrastructure meant to us .h wa:s how do you desi:gn an enterprise so learning isn't left to chance. .hh So that people have the ti::me for learning. .hh people have the resources for learning. .hh People have the occa::sion (.) .h. That learning is part of working. (1.8) Daniel I don't know if you're gonna (0.2) be surprised by this. (0.2) I shouldn't have been because I think I did this a few years ago. (.) .hhh As a matter of just kind of course uh- (.) I should have done this obviously about (0.2) three years ago. .hh I looked up the definition of the word infrastructure this morning.
(0.7) *Looks at document he is holding, closes mouth, pulls up lip corners, shakes head once*
(0.8)

Senge: =Because many people have been telling m- me: I don't know for the last couple of years well this infrastructure doesn't quite kind of capture what you're talking about. .hhh My Websters dictionary said the permanent installations required for military purposes.

Audience: LL[LLLLLLLLLLLLLLLLLLLL-L-L-L-L-L-L-L
[*PS purses his lips and looks at the document from which he has read*

Senge: We have organized a few conferences around this subject of learning infrastructures. .hh I don't think we've ever included a dictionary definition (.) which was probably a bit of a shortcoming on our parts. (0.5) .hhh So: .h you may have to suspend this wor(h)d. .We may have to find a better word. I do not mean the permanent installations required for military operations.=

After summarizing "what infrastructure meant to us" (lines 1–6), Senge indicates that there may be a problem with his use of this concept (lines 6–20). Initially, addressing a colleague, and fellow speaker at the meeting (line 6: "Daniel"), he says that he has looked up a dictionary definition of the term because he has been told that the term does not "quite capture what (he's) talking about" (lines 6–20). Having established a puzzle in the minds of the audience (what *is* the dictionary definition?), he then offers a solution by reading out a dictionary definition which is clearly inconsistent with his use of the term (lines 20–22). This evokes collective laughter by audience members (line 23), the relevance of which Senge confirms by, *inter alia*, falling silent until the laughter ends (lines 23–26). Although he suggests that the dictionary definition may be a source of surprise, Senge does not either announce that the dictionary definition is humorous or smile, laugh, and/or use other recognisably 'comedic' non-verbal techniques as he delivers his message. In contrast to the speakers in Extracts 4.1 and 4.2, Senge initially relies on the content of his message to establish the relevance of audience laughter. He does not use additional cues (pursing his lips and smiling) to signal his humorous intent until after he has completed his message, and a substantial number of audience members have already started to laugh (lines 23–25).

The importance of signalling humorous intent to audience members is underscored by the fact that in all but 2 of the 6 cases in which the onset of audience laughter is staggered the gurus rely on audience members to recognize on the basis of the content of their messages alone that laughter is a relevant, if not an expected, response. Consider Extract 4.4 in which Rosabeth Moss Kanter evokes audience laughter (line 20) after she describes the purported reactions of a number of giant American corporations to a new packaging technology.

After Kanter's description one or two audience members start to laugh.

**Extract 4.4 – "Committee to study it" [GCBA I: 00.21.15]**

Kanter: They were the first producer of fruit and
vegetable juice in the United States (.) to put
their product in the cute little paper bottle.=The
( ) packaging. (0.7) A Well known packaging
technology all over Europe not used in the
United States. I mean again it just shows we're
scouting the world (0.5) for technology including
things like packaging can make a huge difference.
(.) Anyhow they were not known in the United
States. In the early eighties the European manu-
facturers came over (.) to make presentations to
(0.2) to all the food companies to see if they
could interest them in the packaging. (.) So they
make presentations to all of the giants, Coca
Cola, (.) Procter and Gamble etcetera and one
of the gia:nts (0.5) was sufficiently interested in
this that they immediately set up a committee to
study it.
(.)

Audience: L-L[-L-L -L- L- L- L [LLLLLL—L-L-L-L-[L
[ *Expansive smile* [ [

Kanter: [Right (.) uhm [

Kanter: [ Ocean
Spra::y heard the same presentation (0.8)
committed the next da:y, (0.5) signed a deal by
the end of the week, (0.4) and got an eighteen-
month exclusive license.

The absence of an immediate burst of laughter may index, in part, uncertainty on the part of audience members as to whether collective laughter is relevant at this particular juncture. Kanter presents her message in a relatively straightforward way, with the result that the potential relevance of laughter rests largely, if not solely, on the content of her remarks. Subsequently, Kanter confirms that laughter is relevant by not only falling silent but also smiling (line 21). However, the audience members' audible response remains limited to isolated laughter (line 20). In the face of this, Kanter stops smiling and, walking away from the audience, resumes speaking (line 22: "Right"). As she does so, however, additional audience members, start to laugh – possibly in response not only to the preceding isolated laughter but also to Kanter's expansive smile. Kanter hesitates momentarily and then, as the laughter dissolves, goes on to praise the actions of a smaller company called Ocean Spray which, she claims, is not weighed down by bureaucracy (lines 23–27). Examples like this perhaps underline the importance of the cues that gurus routinely use to signal their humorous intent to audience members.

## Confirming/disconfirming the relevance of audience laughter

As Extracts 4.1–4.4 illustrate, in most cases (93) of collective audience laughter, the gurus tacitly confirm the relevance of laughter, regardless of whether it begins with a burst or a 'staggered' onset. Specifically, they cede the floor until the audiences' laughter ends or starts to die away and then, when they resume speaking, they do not assert or otherwise indicate that the audience's laughter was inappropriate or unexpected. When the gurus confirm the relevance of audience laughter, they obviously confirm that their messages were designed to elicit such a response.

However, in 6 cases the gurus do problematize the relevance of audience laughter and thereby cast doubt on the appropriateness of the audiences' treatment of their messages as 'invitations to laugh'. These cases involve the gurus continuing to speak in the face of audience laughter. Consider Extract 4.5 in which Gary Hamel's depiction of construction workers lining up to buy a latte at Starbucks coffee shops elicits audience laughter.

**Extract 4.5 – "Latte at Starbucks" [LinL: 0:38:30]**

Hamel: Now this is not only in kind of high tech
products and it's not only things about the
internet.=Let me give you some very (.)
mundane examples for a moment. (0.4) take
something that certainly in the United States we
all know as a a company Starbucks.=Now
beginning to go interna:tional. (0.7) Who would
have predicted here that you could get
construction workers to line up three deep to
pay two and a half bucks for a latte after all.

Audience: L[L L L L[L L L L L L L L L

Hamel: [Right. [And if- and if I'm sitting there inside
Nestlé running you know the world's largest
coffee brand Nescafe (0.5) how do I feel when in
less than ten years somebody can build a coffee
brand (0.6) that in the largest mar:ket er: coffee
drinking market in the world is a demonstrably
more valuable bra::nd (0.5) than my decades old
coffee brand. (0.5) Does it matter that er Nestlé
grabs a little bit of market share from P and G: in
the (. ) isles of your local supermarket if most of
the new wealth in the coffee business is being
created here.

In contrast to the speakers in Extracts 4.1–4.4 above, Hamel does not cede the floor while the audience members laugh. Having overlapped the onset of their laughter (line 12: "Right"), he starts a new sentence and talks across the remainder of the audiences' response ("And if- and if I'm . . ."), as he initiates a spate of talk which assesses the implications of Starbucks' apparent success in the "coffee business" for its competitor Nestlé. By doing this, Hamel raises the possibility that he may not in fact have invited audience members to laugh and that their laughter was therefore a spontaneous, 'unexpected', 'unlooked for' response.

Although, the gurus sometimes cast doubt on the relevance of audience laughter, there are no examples of them suggesting that their preceding remarks were not, in fact, formulated in humorous terms. With regard to this, recall that audience laughter is not the only way in which audience members can display their understanding that the gurus have said something 'humorous'. Alternative responses include smiling or chuckling quietly, or even silently. In contrast to collective audience laughter, these responses are barely audible and thus do not embody the expectation that the speakers remain silent until they die away. When gurus continue speaking during collective laughter, then, they perhaps problematize not the purportedly humorous character of precipitative messages, but rather the *type* of audience response that is relevant and expected. Atkinson (1984b: 99–105) has argued that when a speaker continues talking in the face of positive audience response it may indicate that it has come as a complete surprise and was not intentionally elicited. Behaving in this way has a number of positive consequences for the speaker. First, it may suggest a spontaneous response on the part of the audience. Second, the speaker demonstrates modesty by not accepting the audience's response. Third, it could suggest that they consider developing their argument or point to be more important than stopping to acknowledge the audience's response. Overall, speaking while being interrupted by an audience may give the impression that the speaker's arguments and message have touched a nerve and that they are in danger of being overwhelmed by the audience's enthusiastic responses.

In summary, collective audience laughter is not simply a spontaneous reaction to messages whose content is self-evidently humorous. Usually, audience laughter is constituted by both gurus and audience members as having been 'invited' by the gurus: the gurus indicate clearly to audience members when laughter is appropriate and expected, and then remain silent until the laughter either ends or begins to die away and when they resume speaking do not suggest that the audience's laughter was inappropriate or unexpected.

## Laughter and applause

As we noted earlier, in three incidents during Tom Peters' lectures laughter is accompanied by clapping on the part of some audience members. In the context of some other forms of public speaking, the co-occurrence of laughter and applause is unexceptional. Thus, for example, in the case of after dinner speeches, stand-up comedy routines and political meetings audiences often clap (as well as laugh) at jokes and quips in order to register appreciation of a speakers wit or originality and/or to display agreement with the underlying messages that speakers are using humour to convey. However, the management gurus' lectures are characteristically akin to various other forms of public speaking, including university lectures and training seminars, in which applause is usually not treated as a relevant activity *either* on its own *or* in conjunction with laughter. In view of this, it is perhaps unsurprising that the incidents of clapping during Peters' lectures occur at points at which Peters is operating at the margins of this genre of public speaking, the type of public speaking that normally characterizes guru lectures. At this blurred boundary individual audience members start to display competing understandings of whether or not applause is relevant. For some he has transgressed the lecturing frame, whereas for others he has not. Let us begin by considering the case in which only a handful of people clap.

**Extract 4.6 – "Paperless toilet" [TOC1: 0.35.20]**

Peters: Two weeks later I got back to the United States,
reading the Wall Street Journal there's an
article, (.) 'Japanese takes to hi-tech bathrooms'
is the title. (0.4) Ten percent of American- of the
market place in Japan is this kind of toilet and it's
a growing activity. (0.2) He says- I'll read you a
sentence (0.2) 'A paperless toilet that sprays
warm water like a bidet except it comes from
several directions. (0.6) Blows warm air to dry
and even sprays scent.

```
Audience: LLL[LLLLL LLLL [LLLLL LLLLLLLLL L-L-[L-L-
TP:            [TP smiles    [                      [And
          that's not all.    [
          L-L-L-L-L-L-L-L=[
Audience:                   [x-x-x-x-x
Audience: =L-[L-L
TP:            [Machine keeps the [seat warm in the Winter.
                                  [TP smiles
Audience: LLLLLLLLL LLLLLLLLLL [LLLLLLLLL
Audience:                      [x-x-x-x
TP:       But that's the world. (0.3) That's the world in
          which people with exotic degrees and no
          degrees have gotta find employment. (0.4)
          That's the world in which companies have got (.)
          to compete.
```

In this case, audience laughter (lines 11–14 and 19) in response to Peters' descriptions of a paperless toilet twice prompts a small number of audience members to applaud (lines 15 and 20). This raises two questions. Why do some audience members (but not others) start to clap? And why doesn't their conduct encourage (via mutual monitoring) a larger number of audience members to applaud? With regard to the first question, it is noticeable that by engaging in humour concerning bodily functions as he describes the hi-tech toilet, Peters adopts a stance which is consistent with that of an 'entertainer' as opposed to an 'educator-who-entertains'. As such, his actions here may appear to be more akin to an after-dinner speech than an educational lecture, and this may be what prompts some audience members to clap, amid the widespread laughter, in order to register appreciation of Peters' wit. As to why others do not clap – although many, if not all, do laugh, it can be suggested that by refraining from applauding the audience display their understanding that applause is not a relevant activity for them to be undertaking during this type of public speaking event. In other words, in contrast to those who clap, the majority of audience members continue to treat laughter-without-applause as the appropriate response. In doing this, they perhaps thereby continue to treat Peters as an 'educator-who-entertains' rather than as an 'entertainer' or, more accurately, as an 'educator' who has, if only momentarily, adopted the stance of an 'entertainer'. Subsequently, Peters unequivocally positions himself as an 'educator' by drawing a serious lesson from his humorous anecdote (lines 20–24).

In the following example a substantial number of audience members applaud in response to Peters' disparaging remarks about inefficient managers.

**Extract 4.7 – "Passing memos" [TOC 3: 39.40]**

TP: What is common (.) is that we are creating a
performance culture around here. (0.4) Now
what does that mean practically?=It means some
things that will probably scare the devil out of
some of you. (0.4) It means such things as, hold
on to your hats and both sides of your seat. (.) It
means getting rid of your pension (0.8) and
replacing it with sharing ten per cent of pre-tax
profits in terms of a performance bonus for
people who do the best work (1.2) An immodest
idea in the United States (.) *(TP stares at a
member of the audience)* to pay people for
performance rather than the number of years
you've kept the seat warm passing memos to
some
[other non-performer.
[*TP looks at notes and walks across stage*

Audience: LLLLLLLLLL LLL[LLLLLLLL LLLLL
[xxx xxxxxxxxxx xxxxxxxxx
xxxxxxxxxx xxxxxxxxxx xxxxxxxxx

(.)

Peters: And in fact (0.4) while I understand (.) the terror
that it should send through a lot of our hearts, (.)
especially er: if you like me share the greyness in
the temples . . .

In delivering his blistering attack on inefficient and complacent managers, Peters departs from the conventional guru practice of deflecting criticism away from audience members. Thus in setting up the message, he suggests that the practical implications of the performance culture that he is advocating "will probably scare the devil out of some of you" (lines 3–5), and advises audience members to "hold on to your hats and both sides of your seat" (lines 5–6). Consequently, the verbal attack on complacent managers is not presented so as to indicate that it does not apply to members of this audience. On the contrary, Peters indicates that the audience probably includes the type of 'non-performer' he is referring to. In view of this it is perhaps not surprising that many members of the audience look decidedly uncomfortable, appear uncertain as to how they should respond, and laugh hesitantly (line 18). Nor is it surprising that this relatively weak spate of audience laughter is quickly superseded by a surge of applause (lines 19–20), which in this context provides individual audience members with a means of unequivocally displaying to Peters, and to each other, that they agree with Peters and thus are not themselves 'non-performers', who would feel threatened by what he has said.

In summary, these examples underline that absence of applause during the gurus' lectures is not predetermined. Instead it would appear to be due in large part to the fact that gurus routinely position themselves as educators-who-entertain rather than as entertainers, and conventionally deflect criticism away from audience members – thus removing the pressure that audience members might otherwise experience to use applause as a means of producing unvarnished displays of affiliation with the gurus in order to publicly exempt themselves from the gurus' criticism.

## Conclusion

We have shown in this chapter that collective audience laughter during management guru lectures is not simply a spontaneous reaction to messages whose content is self-evidently humorous, but rather is evoked by the gurus through the use of a range of interactional practices. Some of these practices are also implicated in the generation of applause by political orators. Thus the gurus use the same non-verbal skills as politicians to stress their messages, and, like politicians, make extensive use of the verbal rhetorical devices discussed by Atkinson (1984a, 1984b) in his influential studies of applause and political oratory. That gurus use contrasts and the like is hardly surprising. As we have noted on several occasions previously, Atkinson (1984a, 1984b) and Heritage and Greatbatch (1986) argue that these devices pervade 'persuasive' talk not only in other forms of public speaking, but also spoken interaction in general. However, our analysis in this chapter also shows that even when the rhetorical devices discussed in CA research are not in evidence in the guru lectures, the speakers use alternative verbal formats which achieve the same ends – namely, emphasizing messages and projecting clear message completion points around which audience members can co-ordinate their responses. Further research is now needed to identify these formats and to determine the extent to which they feature in other forms of public speaking, such as political oratory.

In evoking laughter the gurus also deploy presentational techniques that are specifically related to the evocation of audience laughter. Rather than relying on audience members recognizing that laughter is relevant solely on the basis of the content of their messages, the gurus routinely use a range of non-verbal and, less commonly, verbal cues to signal their humorous intent. These techniques play an important role with respect to the maintenance of publicly displayed shared understandings between gurus and audience members concerning the jocular status of messages and, perhaps, the relevance of collective laughter as opposed to other forms of response (grins, smiles, etc.).

Thus far we have identified a number of generic techniques through which audience laughter is invited and co-ordinated during the gurus' lectures. In the next chapter we turn to examine the role of humour and laughter in the gurus' lectures, paying particular attention to the relationship between audience laughter and the gurus' core ideas and visions. In so doing, we show that, in addition to enhancing the entertainment value of their lectures, the gurus' ability to evoke collective audience laughter enables them to heighten audience attentiveness, to make their messages more memorable, and to orchestrate expressions of group cohesion and solidarity with audience members.

Finally, the strength of such displays of consensus, and the degrees of 'like-mindedness' that they may be taken to index, can vary considerably. Obviously, immediate bursts of laughter (as in Extracts 4.1–4.3 and 4.5) comprise stronger displays of consensus than do laughter episodes whose onsets are staggered and/or delayed (as in Extract 4.4). When the gurus cast doubt on the relevance of laughter (as in Extract 4.5), laughter episodes may display a degree of divergence between the gurus and those audience members who laugh. However, in the present data these displays of disunity are relatively innocuous because the gurus do not go on to indicate that their prior remarks were anything but humorous. More serious are those displays of disunity in which audience members decline to laugh together in response to messages that are formulated by the gurus as invitations to laugh. Even when some or all audience members engage in other forms of affiliative responses, such as smiling or chuckling, these responses may appear weak in the context of messages which (at least retrospectively) appear to have been designed to evoke collective laughter.

Chapter 5

# The role of humour and laughter

In the previous chapter we identified the ways in which management gurus elicit laughter and, very occasionally, applause from their audiences. We now turn to examine the content of the passages that evoked collective audience laughter. Our analysis shows that laughter was restricted to a relatively narrow range of messages. The chapter is therefore organized around a discussion of the following types of messages: praising or criticizing managers and organizations; communicating management ideas without praising or criticizing managers and organizations; referring to potential shortcomings in the gurus' theories; and setting up the delivery of key messages. Additionally, the chapter examines the relationship between the audience laughter these messages evoke and the gurus' core ideas and visions. We question whether all these episodes of laughter can be considered to be unvarnished expressions of support for the ideas gurus express. In doing so, we show how the gurus rarely invite laughter that displays audience members' unequivocal agreement with the latter. Rather, they invest their messages with multiple sources of humour in order to detach the audience's displays of laughter and humour recognition from unambiguous agreement with their core ideas. In concluding, we suggest that this enables them to elicit collective displays of group solidarity, irrespective of whether audience members agree with their core ideas and visions.

## Messages that evoke laughter

An examination of the content of the passages that evoked collective audience laughter shows that laughter was restricted to a relatively narrow range of messages. With a small number of exceptions, the remarks that precipitate laughter fall into four groups. Table 5.1 shows that 64 (65%) of the remarks which precipitate laughter communicate management ideas by praising or criticizing managers and organizations; 14 (14%) communicate management ideas without praising or criticizing managers and organizations; 8 (8%) refer to potential shortcomings in the gurus' theories; and 8 (8%) set up the delivery of key messages. Below, we examine each of these groups of laughter episodes in more detail.

### *Communicating management ideas by praising or criticizing management and organizations*

Often, the gurus extol the virtues of practices that the audience members are unlikely to be using and/or criticize practices that they are likely to be using. However, as we noted in Chapter 3, the gurus are careful to avoid directly criticizing their audiences.

When commending or rejecting organizational practices in these ways, the gurus sometimes evoke audience laughter. Thus, as Table 5.2 shows, 38 per cent (24) of all audience laughter occurs in response to messages that praise the actions, achievements, products or services of third party managers or organizations who are purportedly implementing the organizational theories and

*Table 5.1* Types of remarks that evoke audience laughter

| | *TP* | *RMK* | *PS* | *GH* | *Total* |
|---|---|---|---|---|---|
| Praise/criticize managers/ organizations | 34 | 18 | 6 | 6 | 64 (65%) |
| Management ideas without praise/criticism | 3 | 3 | 5 | 3 | 14 (14%) |
| Potential shortcomings in the gurus' ideas | 3 | 1 | 4 | 0 | 8 (8%) |
| Set up to key messages | 3 | 3 | 1 | 1 | 8 (8%) |
| Other | 0 | 0 | 4 | 1 | 5 (5%) |
| Total | 43 | 25 | 20 | 11 | 99 (100%) |

Note
TP, Tom Peters; RMK, Rosabeth Moss Kanter; PS, Peter Senge; GH, Gary Hamel.

*Table 5.2* The incidence of messages that praise or criticize managers and organizations

| | *TP* | *RMK* | *PS* | *GH* | *Total* |
|---|---|---|---|---|---|
| Praise managers/ organizations, etc. | 15 | 7 | 0 | 2 | 24 (38%) |
| Criticize managers/ organizations, etc. | 19 | 11 | 6 | 4 | 40 (62%) |
| Total | 34 | 18 | 6 | 6 | 64 (100%) |

Note
TP, Tom Peters; RMK, Rosabeth Moss Kanter; PS, Peter Senge; GH, Gary Hamel.

practices that the gurus are advocating. By using humour, the gurus underline the remarkable qualities of the actions, achievements, products or services that they describe. By inviting laughter, they encourage audience members to produce collective displays of affiliation in response to their messages. Consider the example in which Gary Hamel praises the achievements of the coffeeshop chain Starbucks that has adopted the practices he is recommending by elevating coffee into a highly desired product.

**Extract 5.1 – "Latte at Starbucks" [LinL: 0:38:30]**

Hamel: Now this is not only in kind of high tech
products and it's not only things about the
internet.=Let me give you some very (.)
mundane examples for a moment. (0.4) take
something that certainly in the United States we
all know as a a company Starbucks.=Now
beginning to go interna:tional. (0.7) Who would
have predicted here that you could get
construction workers to line up three deep to
pay two and a half bucks for a latte after all.

Audience: L[L L L L[L L L L L L L L

12 Hamel: [Right. [And if- and if I'm sitting there inside
13 Nestlé running you know the world's largest
14 coffee brand Nescafe (0.5) how do I feel when in
15 less than ten years somebody can build a coffee
16 brand (0.6) that in the largest mar:ket er: coffee
17 drinking market in the world is a demonstrably
18 more valuable bra::nd (0.5) than my decades old
19 coffee brand. (0.5) Does it matter that er Nestlé
20 grabs a little bit of market share from P and G: in
21 the (.) aisles of your local supermarket if most of
22 the new wealth in the coffee business is being
23 created here.

Hamel's rhetorical question in lines 7–10 illustrates the purported success of Starbucks by describing how construction workers queue to buy lattes from their outlets and depicting this as an extraordinary and unforeseen achievement ("Who would have predicted . . ."). Having evoked a collective display of affiliation (line 11), Hamel reverts to a serious stance as he refers to the implications of Starbucks' success in the 'coffee business' for its competitor Nestlé on their well-established Nescafe brand (lines 12–23). It is noticeable that Hamel selects as the target of his humorous remark a brand that will be well known to the audience. Few in the audience will not have come across their retail outlets or advertising. Furthermore, it is associated with success and excellence and innovativeness in retail practice. The example powerfully illustrates his key point that organizations need to be revolutionary and reinvent their market. By implication, if one of the oldest established and highest profile brands is being threatened by the popularity of a new way of selling coffee then potentially no product is safe from the reinvention of customer expectations.

In the following example, Tom Peters praises a motor vehicle that is purportedly a product of the customer-focussed management practices he is recommending to the audience members.

**Extract 5.2 – "Ford Taurus" [TPE1:00:19:00]**

Peters: And that's the way customers make judgements of things in general.=Look at the other side of it though.=The delight si:de. (0.4) About a year or so ago: when we had some friends visiting us in California where I live, (0.4) I'd been reading about all this marvelous success that the Ford Taurus is having (.) and so I rented one because I want to try one and see what it was li:ke. (.) (1.0) In two minutes I'd fell in love with the Ford Taurus. (.) You won't be surprised at the reason given the story I just told you. (0.5) In twenty-nine years of driving automobiles it is the first car I have ever driven that has a place to put the coffee cup.

Audience: LLLLLLLLLLLLLLL

Peters: Five billion dollar development project (.) for Fo:rd. (.) And I refer to the whole damn car as the coffee cup car. (.) Which is what it is to me. And that's the way people make decisions.

Trading off his earlier admission (not included in the extract) that he is 'physiologically addicted' to coffee and needs caffeine early in the morning (see Extract 5.9 and story in Extract 6.10), Peters evokes audience laughter in response to a message which reveals a trivial reason, the provision of a coffee cup holder, for his positive reaction to a motor vehicle, the Ford Taurus (lines 5–14). In doing so, he stresses both how remarkable the vehicle is, in that it is unique in his experience to have this feature, and how idiosyncratic customers can be. In this way, he substantiates his contention that managers must take account of the apparently insignificant needs of customers and clients.

As Table 5.2 shows, 62 per cent (40) of all laughter episodes occur in response to messages that criticize managers/organizations for employing practices that the gurus reject.[1] In these cases, the gurus' use of humour underlines the inappropriateness of commonplace management practices. Consider the following example in which Kanter derides the purportedly slow bureaucratic reactions of a number of giant American corporations to a new packaging technology.

**Extract 5.3 – "Committee to study it" [GCBA 1: 00.21.15]**

Kanter: They were the first producer of fruit and
vegetable juice in the United States (.) to put
their product in the cute little paper bottle.=The
( ) packaging. (0.7) A Well known packaging
technology all over Europe not used in the
United States. I mean again it just shows we're
scouting the world (0.5) for technology including
things like packaging can make a huge difference.
(.) Anyhow they were not known in the United
States. In the early eighties the European manu-
facturers came over (.) to make presentations to
(0.2) to all the food companies to see if they
could interest them in the packaging. (.) So they
make presentations to all of the giants, Coca
Cola, (.) Procter and Gamble etcetera. And one
of the gia:nts (0.5) was sufficiently interested in
this that they immediately set up a committee to
study it.
(.) *Slight head tilt; closes lips slightly and smiles;*
*holds head still for a moment*

Audience: LL[LL L- L- L- L [LLLLLLLLL LLLL-L-[L
[*Expansive smile* [ [

Kanter: [Right (.) uhm [

Kanter: [Ocean Spra::y heard the same
presentation (0.8) committed the next da:y, (0.5)
signed a deal by the end of the week, (0.4) and
got an eighteen-month exclusive license.

By using humour and inviting audience members to laugh, Kanter highlights the purported absurdity of the reactions of the giant corporations to the presentations made by the European manufacturers. By laughing, audience members display their appreciation of Kanter's humour and incongruous imagery. Following the audience's laughter, Kanter reverts to a serious stance as she stops smiling and praises the actions of a smaller company called Ocean Spray that she claims is not weighed down by bureaucracy.

In the following example, Peter Senge intensifies his criticism of bureaucratic structures that impede organizational learning by disparaging universities.

**Extract 5.4 – "Universities" [FD: 0.15.35]**

Senge: Look at- .hh (.) I: live in an organization (0.2)
who's dedicated to science right?
(2.2) *Wide-eyed expression, mouth open*
So if in any organization it would be ea:sy: (.) to
display one's ignorance (0.2) or one's incom-
plete thinking it would be a university right? .hh
How many of you have ever worked in uni-
versities.
(1.2) *Looks around audience, mouth slightly open; after about half a second he raises his hand*
D'you think they are characterized any less so by
contro:l?
(0.2) *Closes mouth, slight smile*

14 Audience: LLLLLLLLL LLLLLL[LLL

15 Senge: [Some people would even
16 [*Stops smiling*
17 argue more so.

By using humour and evoking laughter, Senge underlines the purported inappropriateness of universities adopting organizational structures that impede learning (lines 11–12). The humorous comment juxtaposes the role of universities as institutions that are intended to encourage and facilitate learning with their often unwieldy bureaucratic structures that can stifle learning. In this respect his comment is presented as an incongruity. As the audience's laughter (line 14) subsides, Senge ceases smiling and adopts a 'serious' stance, as he develops his criticism of universities.

In summary, by using humour and inviting the audience members to laugh in response to messages that praise or criticize third-party managers and organizations, the gurus emphasize either the positive or negative aspects of the achievements, actions, products or services they describe. The data contain a larger proportion of negative than positive cases. There is therefore a tendency for gurus when they make evaluations of a state of affairs to be more critical than praising. This tendency to negativity in public speaking has been noted before (see Heritage and Greatbatch, 1986: 121). Drawing on Simmel (1902), Greatbatch and Heritage argue that this may arise because the potential attitudes audience members have to a statement may be very different. Since individuals tend to agree more with negative statements a unified response is more likely when such statements are deployed.

All of these laughter episodes involve the gurus formulating a situation as surprising and or unusual, and inviting audience members to laugh and thereby exhibit agreement with their values (standards of judgement) concerning some aspect of social life. In a very few cases (3), this involves the gurus offering audience members opportunities to express (through laughter) unvarnished support for the values that are embedded in their core management ideas and visions. Consider Extract 5.3 on page 90 in which Moss

Kanter evokes laughter in response to her depiction of the reactions of a large corporation to an innovative packaging technology. To a large extent, the humour of her remarks, which are produced 'straight-faced' with no humorous elaboration, derives from acceptance of her espoused view that most organizations are too bureaucratic, too conservative, and too cautious when they encounter innovatory practices and products. Consequently, given the absence of other potential sources of humour, the audience's laughter may be interpreted as expressing support for her point of view concerning organizational practice in general.

In the vast majority of cases (96), however, the gurus do *not* construct and deliver their messages so as to invite audiences to produce, through laughter, unvarnished expressions of support for values that derive from their core ideas and visions. Thus, for example, the gurus frequently invest their messages with multiple sources of humour. This is starkly illustrated by comparing Moss Kanter's critique of bureaucratic organizations in Extract 5.3 with that of Tom Peters, which we first considered in Chapter 4 (Extract 4.1) and is reproduced in Extract 5.5 below:

**Extract 5.5 – "When you see a snake" [TOC2: 35.56]**

| | | |
|---|---|---|
| TP: | | My favourite Perroism of all was his description, right before leaving GM, of |
| | | what he sa:w as the difference between Electronic Data Systems and GM. (0.6) He said, |
| | | ["At EDS (.) WHEN YOU SEE A SNAKE |
| | | [*Leans forward, glares, uses angry tone of voice* |
| | | (.) YOU KILL IT". |
| Audience: | → | [LLLLLLLLL LLLLLLLLL LLLLLL-L-L-L |
| | | [*Turns and walks* |

| | | |
|---|---|---|
| Peters: | | [He said, "At GM when you see a snake,<br>[you search the world for the top<br>[*Leans forward/smile face*<br>consultant on snakes. |
| Audience: | → | LLLLLLLLL LLLLLLLLL |
| Peters: | | Then you appoint a committee on snakes and you study snakes for the next two years. (1.0) <Flat (.) fluid (.) and get on with it (.) that':s the creature. |

Here Peters evokes laughter in response to his (and Perot's) praise of the supposedly rapid reaction of one organization, and criticism of the purportedly slow reactions of another. In so doing, Peters conveys a critique of big, 'bureaucratic' organizations that closely resembles the stance taken by Kanter in Extract 5.3 on page 90. However, in this instance there are several other potential sources of humour in addition to the critique *per se*. These include Perot's metaphorical imagery and style of speaking, and Peters's mimicry of these. Consequently, individual audience members may be displaying their appreciation of the humour in these features, as opposed to (or in addition to) Perot's evaluation of the corporations' actions and, by extension, Peters's core ideas. This means that while audience members' engage in collective displays of affiliation with Peters, their laughter does not represent *unvarnished* expressions of support for the position he is using the Perot quotation to substantiate. Thus, by offering multiple sources of humour speakers are able to invest their remarks with considerable affiliative potential by permitting participants to hold multiple understandings of the situation but display these as a unified response.

As Extracts 5.1 and 5.2 illustrate, the gurus also frequently invite audience members to laugh at the byproducts of the organizational practices they are recommending or criticizing, rather than at the practices themselves. Thus, for example, in Extract 5.1, the target of

Gary Hamel's humour is a purportedly surprising aspect of the success of a coffeeshop chain strategy (construction workers queuing for a latte) which has apparently adopted his ideas by recreating the market for coffee; while in Extract 5.2 the 'target' of Peters' humour is his praise of a small detail of a car (a coffee cup holder) which has been produced by a company that is purportedly adopting the customer-focused strategy he is advocating. Consequently, although audience members exhibit that they share Hamel's perspective concerning the popularity of a product among a particular occupational group, and Peters' perspective concerning his reaction to a small detail of a car, their laughter clearly does not represent an unvarnished expression of support for the gurus' core, underlying management ideas.

In summary, by using humour and inviting the audience members to laugh in response to messages that praise or criticize third-party managers and organizations, the gurus emphasize either the positive or negative aspects of the achievements, actions, products or services they describe. In so doing, however, they rarely offer audience members opportunities to express or decline to express unequivocal support for their core management ideas. Instead, they invest their messages with multiple sources of humour and/or invite displays of affiliation with values that do not derive directly from their core management ideas and visions. The fact that the gurus routinely 'play safe' by inviting audience laughter which is *not* open to interpretation as an unvarnished expression of support for their core positions is perhaps not surprising. The gurus often recommend/praise practices that audience members are unlikely to be using and criticize practices that audience members are likely to be using (Greatbatch and Clark, 2002). Although managers may welcome exposure to ideas that question what they do, it does not follow that they will wish to affiliate publicly with them. By inviting audience laughter that is not open to interpretation as an unvarnished expression of support for their core ideas, the gurus may, among other things, increase their chances of generating affiliative exchanges with audience members, even if these conditions apply.

### *Communicating management ideas without praising or criticising the achievements, action or services of managers and organizations*

Table 5.1 shows that the gurus evoked laughter on 14 occasions (14 per cent of all laughter episodes) in response to messages which communicate their management ideas without directly praising or criticizing the achievements, actions, products or services of managers and organizations. In eight of these cases the gurus convey their management ideas either by reference to non-management contexts or without reference to management contexts. These occur in lectures given by Rosabeth Moss Kanter (2), Peter Senge (5) and Gary Hamel (1). In the following example, Gary Hamel tells an unattributed story about Nikita Khrushchev's maiden speech as president of the Soviet Union, during which he denounced the crimes of his predecessor, Joseph Stalin. Hamel uses the story to illustrate his point that it is difficult to promote change in organizations.

**Extract 5.6 – "Khrushchev" [LinL: 01:05:00]**

Hamel: And it takes courage. (1.0) You know being an activist is not an easy thing. (0.7) There's a- there's a wonderful story uh- (.) when when ( ) Khrushchev took over the supreme soviet (0.8) his maiden speech (0.5) er he used it to denounce the crimes of Stalin. (0.7) And he went through this litany of horrors that- that Stalin had perpetrated on the Soviet Union. (0.8) And er (.) half way through this lo:ng speech somebody sitting at the back of this huge auditorium shouted out a question. (0.6) he said Comrade Khrushchev you were there you were with Stalin why didn't you stop him. (1.1) Khrushchev looked at him and said >who said

| | |
|---|---|
| | that<. (0.8) No hand went up. Right. (0.3) He said now you know why:. [Right.= |
| | [*Dips head and raises and lowers eyebrows* |
| Audience: | L-LLLLLLLLL LL[L L L L L L - L - L |
| Hamel: | [Think about it. |
| Hamel: | So it does take some courage. |

In the other 6 cases the gurus convey their views concerning the changing nature of either work or the environment in which organizations operate. These occur in lectures given by Tom Peters (2), Rosabeth Moss Kanter (1), Peter Senge (1) and Gary Hamel (2). In the following example, Peters twice evokes audience laughter in response to a joke that he attributes to an unnamed academic. The joke uses incongruous imagery to refer to the impact that auto-pilot systems will have on the role of commercial airline pilots in the future. Peters uses the joke to illustrate his contention that organizations and individuals must adapt to constantly changing environments.

**Extract 5.7 – "Auto-pilot Systems" [TPE1:0:04:40]**

| | |
|---|---|
| Peters: | And s- issues number one relative to this customer orientation customer obsession (.) customer revolution (0.3) is that everyone had best be [inventing (.) creating and recreating (.) markets with extraordinary regularity. (1.0) [(.) In fact the best description of how these times are changing I think was er- was one I ran across the other da:y, this is a comment from a University of Miami Professor of Management Science, (.) |

| | |
|---|---|
| | [addressing the Airlines Pilot's Association (.) describing |
| | [*looks up from notes, slight smile* |
| | the aero (.) plane (0.2) of the year two thousand and five. (0.5) He said the crew will consist of one pilot and a do:g. (1.5) The pilot will be there to nurture and [feed the dog, |
| | [ *Looks at audience* |
| Audience: | [L-LLLLLLLLLL |
| | [*Looks at notes, closes mouth, smiles* |
| Peters: | the do:g will be there to bite the pilot (.) |
| | [if he tries to touch anything. |
| | [*Smiles* |
| Audience: | LLLLLLLL |

In these cases, then, gurus produce humorous remarks that substantiate their management ideas without explicitly praising or disparaging managers or organizations. Although the gurus may imply that audience members, and managers in general, have failed to recognize the importance of the phenomena they describe, the gurus do not directly criticize them for this neglect. In this way, the gurus minimize the risk that the audience members will react negatively to their messages. Indeed, structuring their comments in this way offers a number of levels of insulation from potentially negative reactions. The comments are presented as humorous and so not intended to offend. By obtaining collective laughter the audience confirm this understanding and at the same time the gurus are endorsed as speaking on behalf of the audience. Apart from bolstering the gurus' ideas, these humorous remarks, like those discussed in the previous section, allow audience members to publicly affiliate with the gurus, without having to unequivocally align with their propositions. They therefore permit an ambiguity to exist but not be publicly displayed. Finally, these humorous remarks do not concern management and so cannot be characterized as a comment on the capabilities and skills of those present.

### *References to potential shortcomings in the gurus' ideas*

Perhaps understandably, the gurus rarely risk undermining their own credibility by considering possible shortcomings in their work. Nonetheless, eight per cent (8) of the instances of audience laughter occur in situations in which the gurus refer to potential problems in their theories. These occur in lectures given by Tom Peters (3), Rosabeth Moss Kanter (1) and Peter Senge (4). Consider the example in which Peter Senge accepts that a concept (infrastructure) that has been central to his theory about organizational learning is inappropriate. It is likely that Senge addressed this issue because it was in the public domain at the time of his lecture.

**Extract 5.8 – "Infrastructure" [FD: 0.48.50]**

(Discussing co-edited volume: *The Fifth Discipline Field Book*)

Senge: So what infrastructure meant to us .h wa:s how
do you desi:gn an enterprise so learning isn't left
to chance. .hh So that people have the ti::me for
learning. .hh people have the resources for
learning. .hh People have the occa::sion (.) .h.
That learning is part of working. (1.8) Daniel I
don't know if you're gonna (0.2) be surprised by
this. (0.2) I shouldn't have been because I think I
did this a few years ago. (.) .hhh ^As a matter of
just kind of course uh- (.) I should have done this
obviously about (0.2) three years ago. .hh I
looked up the definition of the word infra-
structure this morning.
(0.7) *Looks at document he is holding, closes mouth,*
*pulls up lip corners, shakes head once*
(0.8)

Senge: =Because many people have been telling m- me: I
don't know for the last couple of years well this
infrastructure doesn't quite kind of capture what

you're talking about. .hhh My Websters dictionary said the permanent installations required for military purposes.

Audience: LL[LLLLLLLLLLLLLLLLLLLLL-L-L-L-L-L-L-L
[*PS purses his lips and looks at the document from which he has read*

Senge: We have organized a few conferences around this subject of learning infrastructures. .hh I don't think we've ever included a dictionary definition (.) which was probably a bit of a shortcoming on our parts. (0.5) .hhh So: .h you may have to suspend this wor(h)d. .We may have to find a better word. I do not mean the permanent installations required for military operations.=

After describing "what infrastructure meant to us" (lines 1–6), Senge indicates that there is a problem with his use of this concept (lines 6–20). He says that he has looked up a dictionary definition of the term because people have been telling him for some time that the term doesn't "quite capture what (he's) talking about". He then reads out a dictionary definition that is clearly absurd in relation to his use of the term (lines 20–22). This evokes collective laughter by audience members (line 23). Having treated the issue as humorous, Senge then addresses it in serious terms (lines 26–34). The importance that Senge attaches to this issue is demonstrated by the fact that he returns to it when concluding his lecture and, in doing so, again treats it as a 'serious' matter.

By treating shortcomings in their work as humorous, the gurus exhibit that they are in a position to take them lightly. By doing so, they propose that they do not regard the shortcomings to be of critical importance. And, by inviting laughter, they encourage the audience members to publicly ratify their treatment of the shortcomings in humorous terms. However, once again the gurus do not evoke unvarnished expressions of support with their core ideas and visions. Thus, while audience members in Extract 5.8 display a shared perspective with Peter Senge concerning the purported absurdity of a dictionary definition of the term infrastructure (in relation to his use of the term), their laughter does not represent an unequivocal expression of support for his core message, namely that his decision to discard this term, which was previously at the heart of his theory of organizational learning, is not of great significance.

In the preceding sections we have examined the role of humour and laughter in the communication of the gurus' ideas. This accounts for 87 per cent (86) of laughter episodes. In the majority of them (78), gurus convey ideas that might imply criticism of audience members, although they are careful not to directly address this possibility. In the remaining cases (8) the gurus deal with issues that might be deemed problematic for themselves. Apart from enabling the gurus to underscore the positive or negative aspects of particular states of affairs, the use of humour and the elicitation of audience laughter assists the gurus in dealing with the potentially negative aspects of either audience-directed or self-directed criticism. In the case of audience-directed criticism, the gurus provide audience members with opportunities to affiliate with them in contexts in which they could be seen to be implicitly criticizing the audience. This generates affiliative exchanges between the gurus and their audiences, even though audiences are not required to publicly display their support for the gurus' ideas. This enables the gurus to deliver potentially unpalatable messages in a positive climate. In the case of guru-directed criticism, the gurus use humour to present problematic issues concerning their ideas as suitable for light-hearted treatment and therefore as manageable. By inviting audience laughter, they encourage audience members to produce collective displays of affiliation that exhibit appreciation of, and ratify, their humorous treatment of the issues in question. Again, this allows the gurus to deliver potentially problematic messages (in this case for them rather than audience members) in affiliative contexts.

### *Setting up key messages*

Eight per cent (8) cases of audience laughter are evoked by remarks that gurus make while preparing to deliver key messages. These occur in lectures given by Tom Peters (3), Rosabeth Moss Kanter (3), Peter Senge (1) and Gary Hamel (1), and pave the way for messages concerning management practice. In the following extract, Tom Peters sets up a story about the poor service he received at a hotel by announcing that he is going to reveal to his audience "two personal habits" (lines 1–3), and in doing so evokes audience laughter (line 4).

**Extract 5.9 – "Two personal habits" [TPE1: 0.19.00]**

Peters: Now (0.5) I will er: reveal to you two personal
habits that are none of your damn business
basically.

Audience: LLLLLLLLL
(0.5)

Peters: One of them is that I do my writing (0.6) by
getting up about four o'clock in the morning
(0.5) and the second one is that if we had a
physician (0.8) at this conference he or she
would probably be able to classify me as
physiologically addicted (0.8) to coffee.

Another case occurs in one of Senge's lectures in which he elicits laughter while setting up a message concerning general theories that are not explicitly linked to management. In the following extract he asks the audience a rhetorical question and unexpectedly elicits laughter. We shall discuss the implications of this later in the chapter.

**Extract 5.10 – "The word theory" [FD: 0.13.00]**

Senge: And then we do: (.) what I think is the essence of
what a scientific community as- (.) aspires to

do::. .hh We make our thinking public. (0.8)
[Which is [ really
[*Pulls up lip corners*
[*Wide eyed expression*
humbling [hehm=
[*Closes mouth/smiles*

Audience: [= L- [ L-L-L-L-L
[Opens [mouth, continues to smile------------>]

Senge: [If you thought about something before::]
.hh where you're just building a model going
jee:z (0.8) is this how it works? (.) I think it's how
it works. .hhh Then you actually show it to
somebody. (0.7) .hh D'you know (that) the word
theory: has the same roots as the (.) theatre?
(0.7) *Looks around the audience, eyes wide, mouth*
*slightly open*

Audience: L-L-L-L-[L-L-L

Senge: [It's true It's a Greek term theorea. .h It
means to kind of la:y out in the open, .h to
displa:y.

Apart from the provision of 'entertainment' and 'light relief', the use of humour in these contexts may both attract the audience members' attention prior to the delivery of key messages and establish an affiliative context prior to the delivery of messages that could implicate audience-directed criticism. In addition, as the extract from the Tom Peters' lecture shows, the humour may also address potentially problematic aspects of what follows. Thus the two personal habits to which Peters refers are: (1) that he gets up at 4am to write and (2) that he is addicted to coffee. Having evoked laughter in response to his announcement that he is going to reveal these habits (lines 1–4), Peters adopts a serious stance as he discusses them (lines 6–11). By eliciting laughter he has: (1) guarded against the possibility that he will be heard by audience members to be revealing habits that he regards as serious problems and (2) encouraged the audience to publicly display, through collective laughter, that they are aware of this. In other words, Peters appears to use humour and laughter to, *inter alia*, nullify the potentially face-threatening aspects of revealing one's 'personal habits'.

In summary, gurus sometimes evoke laughter in the course of setting up the delivery of key messages. In addition to attracting the audiences' attention, the gurus may also establish an affiliative context and, in some cases, an appropriate interpretative framework for what follows. Even in these cases, then, humour and laughter may be critical to the delivery and reception of the gurus' ideas.

## Conclusion

The gurus evoke laughter in response to a relatively narrow range of messages: praising or criticizing managers and organizations; communicating management ideas without praising or criticizing managers and organizations; referring to potential shortcomings in their theories; and setting up the delivery of key messages. With three exceptions, the gurus construct and deliver their messages in ways that disengage humour recognition from their core ideas and/or invest their messages with multiple sources of humour. By so doing, they delineate those aspects of social life in relation to which audience laughter may express shared values and norms, and vary the extent to which audience laughter is open to interpretation as an unvarnished expression of support for their core management ideas.

Together with the techniques examined in Chapter 4, these presentational devices play an important role in the gurus' communication of their ideas and visions, especially in relation to the management of group cohesion and solidarity during their lectures. Studies of humour and laughter in a variety of social contexts suggest that it can promote the emergence and maintenance of group cohesiveness by, *inter alia*, clarifying and reinforcing shared values and social norms; disciplining those who violate the rules of a social group, and unifying other group members against them; and dividing group members from other groups (those who would be expected to adopt a different perspective; see, for example, Meyer,

2000). It is unclear whether the gurus and their audiences can be classified as members of distinctive social groups. Indeed, part of the management gurus' mission is to recruit managers to such groups, whose boundaries are defined by reference to their members' affiliation with the gurus' theories. Nonetheless, by evoking and producing laughter, the gurus and their audience members engage in public displays of consensus and 'like-mindedness' (Glenn, 1989) and thereby *constitute* themselves as 'in-groups' that share a common perspective in relation to the circumstances and events that the gurus describe. When gurus attack/disparage others (e.g. Extract 5.3), as opposed to emphasizing the positive qualities of a supposedly unusual situation (e.g. Extract 5.1), the gurus and those audience members who laugh also publicly differentiate themselves from individuals or groups who purportedly do not share the values or perspectives they are expressing. In these cases, then, humour and laughter delineate group boundaries by acting as both a unifier and divider (Meyer, 2000).

Whether these publicly displayed group affiliations actually reflect audience members' commitment to the gurus' views and thus may extend beyond the lifetime of the gurus' lectures is, of course, open to question. Nonetheless, even those very few cases of laughter that are not open to interpretation as unvarnished expressions of support for the gurus' core ideas indicate a shared perspective and – like affiliative interactional practices in general (Goffman, 1983; Heritage, 1984) – contribute to a sense of cohesion and intimacy, which might make audiences more receptive to the gurus' recommendations. Moreover, conversation analytic research on public speaking suggests that the effective use of humour by gurus may have a positive impact on their ability to win and retain 'converts'. Thus Atkinson's (1984a, 1984b) studies of the generation of applause during political speeches demonstrate that certain rhetorical devices (e.g. contrast, lists and puzzle–solution formats), when used effectively, attract and sustain audience attentiveness to what is being said and thereby contribute to the memorability of the speaker's messages. This is because the devices make messages stand out from surrounding speech materials and, in some cases, evoke audience applause, which, in turn, heightens audience attentiveness and contributes to the prominence of the message. Humorous messages stand out from their surroundings, irrespective of whether or not other rhetorical devices are used. Moreover, just as applause enhances the prominence of preceding messages, so do other forms of collective audience response, including laughter. Given that speakers are unlikely to persuade audiences to empathize with their positions unless they sustain the attentiveness of audience members, it seems likely that humour is one means through which gurus and other public speakers create the conditions necessary to win and retain converts.

Chapter 6

# Telling stories

Stories are an important feature of all the gurus' lectures. Indeed, as we indicated in Chapter 3, the gurus' lectures can be characterized as a collection of ideas illustrated by reference to a series of stories that relate to, but may not be about, organizational life. In some cases, the lectures are projected from the outset as storytelling events. The audience is informed that they are there to listen to the guru's ideas and a series of anecdotal stories that illustrate their points. Thus, for example, Tom Peters opens his *Service with Soul* lecture as follows:

*Peters*: Well it is a great pleasure to have a chance to chat with you about some extraordinary stories, but, before doing that what I would like to do is to put it in a context which in my opinion is incredibly serious, particularly for those of you in the corporate world. The last 10 or 15 years have been volatile and that's an understatement.

The importance of stories in guru presentations has been previously recognized by Clark and Salaman (1998) who argued that a major reason for management gurus' appeal to managers is their ability to constitute the world they describe, and the key 'players' in that corporate world, in the form of compelling stories during their live presentations. They suggest that management gurus' success with managers is related to their capacity 'to address and manipulate through myths and stories, symbolic issues of great pertinence and salience to senior managers: senior managers' own roles, skills and identities within the "new" organization' (p. 149). In doing so, they define the dispositions, actions and attributes that constitute successful management. They do this by conveying their ideas and expertise to managers through language and in particular the telling of powerful stories. Their tales are of miraculous strategic virtuosity, of heroic turnarounds, of battles with organizational monsters (poor quality, poor service levels, huge inventory levels, etc.), and above all about the necessary virtues for organizational success. Above all they are about the heroes and heroines who make success possible – the new manager. Clark and Salaman, therefore, conceive of gurus as master storytellers whose tales appeal to and resonate with managers because they centre on and celebrate the management role by offering 'a conception of management itself in virtuous, heroic, high status terms' (p. 157).

The notion that a key reason for the gurus' reputations as powerful orators is the stories they tell is therefore prominent within the literature on management gurus. Indeed, it is so frequently mentioned that it has become a commonly accepted fact. But, as we stated in Chapter 2, previous studies of the guru phenomenon are founded upon a conceptual rather than empirically-based understanding of their live presentations. Claims about the storytelling prowess of gurus and the nature of the stories they tell are based more on assertion than empirically-derived evidence. Consequently, our knowledge of the extent to which gurus are storytellers, the prominence of stories in relation to other segments of talk, the nature of the stories they tell and, the possible functions of stories within their talk, is very partial. In this chapter we examine each of these issues based on our analysis of the four gurus' lectures. We begin by reviewing the literature that has sought to define the nature of stories and by setting out our approach to identifying the stories in the gurus' lectures. Following this we examine how management gurus project the onset of stories to their audiences and the implications this has for audience attentiveness. We then consider how the gurus formulate their stories in order to (1) illustrate their ideas and visions, (2) reinforce the authority of their knowledge and (3) create and enhance their 'star' status.

## What is a story?

What does and does not constitute a story has generated considerable controversy and debate. This issue is exemplified by Boje's (1991) seminal study of organizational storytelling in which he identified 11 story-line patterns from an analysis of 100 hours of taped recordings in an office supply firm. Boje's (1991: 112–113) main finding was that 'the storytelling did not appear in concise sequences of storytellers recounting full texts to passive listeners . . . people told their stories in bits and pieces, with excessive interruptions of story starts, with people talking over each other to share story fragments, and many aborted storytelling attempts'. Since the storytelling process was not a continuous event he labelled the story fragments he collected as 'terse'. Their meaning was only accessible to those familiar with the events to which the stories refer since the hearer has to fill-in-the-blanks. So long as the teller and hearer share a common understanding about the nature of the events being relayed a signalling phrase was enough to convey the whole story. Boje (1991: 115) therefore asks the question 'just how abbreviated can a story be and still be classified as a story?' His answer is that the utterance 'You know the story' is the shortest story. A detailed narration of the actual events is not necessary since both parties appreciate which story is being evoked in the current context. It is not so much a telling as a request on the part of one person for another to access a shared narrative. This short utterance can therefore convey an enormous amount of narrative detail without a full elaboration being required.

Boje's is an extreme position. At the other end of the continuum are authors such as Gabriel (2000: 20–21) who argue that Boje's 'terse' stories are nothing more than 'delicate fragments of sense' and 'coded left-overs from impoverished narratives' which break the conventionally-accepted notions of the nature of a story. For Gabriel (2000) stories have beginnings, middles and ends, and are held together by action and characters. He therefore defines stories as:

> narratives with plots and characters, generating emotion in narrator and audience through a poetic elaboration of symbolic

> material . . . Story plots entail conflicts, predicaments, trials, coincidences, and crises that call for choices, decisions, actions and interactions, whose actual outcomes are often at odds with the characters' intentions and purposes.
>
> (Gabriel, 2000: 239)

In a similar vein Thompson (1990: 288) writes that a story 'generally consists of a constellation of characters and a succession of events, combined in a way which displays a certain orientation to "plot"'. From this perspective a story is a plot which is comprised of a sequential series of events, which may or may not follow in chronological order, but are tied together by actions and characters. In this sense, Boje's (1991) stories are proto-stories in that some of these elements are absent because they represent an incomplete simplification of the story in which parts of the plot, some of the characters, and segments of the sequence of events are excluded because they are 'left to the hearer's imagination' (Boje, 1991: 115).

Despite apparent differences, the 'terse' and 'elaborate' approaches to the definition of stories nevertheless adopt a common method in that they attempt to develop a priori formal definitions which are then applied to data to determine what will and will not be counted as a story for the purposes of the research. In other words, they privilege the researcher's rather than the speaker's view of what constitutes a story. We wish to pursue an alternative approach that circumvents these definitional issues. This involves us focusing on segments of talk that the speaker (i.e. guru) identifies as stories in their speech. These may be 'terse' depictions of events, situations and happenings in that they comprise single, fragmented sentences, or they may be elaborate and extended narratives that unfold over many sentences and several minutes. Whichever type of story is told, the critical point for us is that the speaker produces a segment of talk that is recognizable and hearable as a story. The gurus have to indicate that they are about to tell a story so that the members of audience hear what is being presented as a story. So, for us a segment of talk that is classifiable as a 'story' is projected as a story by the teller so that it comes off as a story for the hearer. We now turn to discuss how the gurus established the onset of a story for their audiences.

## The nature of gurus' stories

When the gurus tell a story they do so in such a way that it is clearly differentiated from foregoing speech matter. The gurus produce speech fragments that are recognizable and hearable as stories by inferring to the audience that their next communicative act is intended as a story so that the audience hears what is subsequently presented as a story. They achieve this by using a 'story preface'. In everyday conversation, story prefaces are important because, as a number of conversation analytic studies have shown, in normal turn-by-turn conversation storytelling is a project (Jefferson, 1978; Ryave, 1978; Sacks, 1995). It is something that has to be achieved because the telling of a story involves 'an attempt to control the floor over an extended series of utterances' (Sacks, 1995: 18). Telling a story necessitates that someone has to speak and hold the audience's attention for a number of sentences (i.e. beyond the length of a usual utterance). Rather than formally asking for permission to speak for a longer turn we signal that we wish to do so through the use of a story preface. A story preface is an utterance that indicates the teller is going to talk for an extended period and at the same time links the relevance of the story to the surrounding talk. It also provides recipients with key resources that they can use to analyse the story as it is being told in that it offers an initial characterization of what the story will be about and indicates that what is going to be said will be of interest to the listeners. For example, if the preface states that the story will be about something "terrible" recipients can monitor the unfolding of the story so that they identify the points of climax and completion. If the telling of a humorous story is indicated then the audience will know that it is not to be taken seriously and that at some point laughter may be expected. A story preface therefore does a lot of work. Most critically it indicates the onset of a story and at the same time promises it will be interesting, thus increasing the incentive for the listeners to pay attention to the next passage of talk.

As in normal conversation the gurus use story prefaces to announce that they are about to tell a story. Using the definition we developed in the previous section, Table 6.1 shows that a total of 52 stories were told in these lectures. Peters told 12 stories (23%),

*Table 6.1* Incidence of stories in the gurus' lectures

| | *TP* | *RMK* | *PS* | *GH* | *Total* |
|---|---|---|---|---|---|
| Number of stories | 12 | 16 | 12 | 12 | 52 |

Note
TP, Tom Peters; RMK, Rosabeth Moss Kanter; PS, Peter Senge; GH, Gary Hamel.

Kanter 16 (31%), Senge 12 (23%), and Hamel 12 (23%). The stories account for 18.3 per cent of total talk time and range in length from a little under 20 seconds to over 4 minutes. The great majority (87%) of the topics of the stories are about commonplace, familiar and mundane activities that are unlikely to excite much interest from the audience. These included eating at a restaurant, checking-in to a hotel, travelling on some form of transportation, filling a car with petrol, test driving a car, buying a shirt, attending a management meeting and so forth. Kanter tells 7 (13%) stories that are about unusual and out-of-the-ordinary activities. Several of these occur in an extended extract featured later in the chapter. In two of her lectures (Lessons in Leadership and Managing Change) she tells a series of stories about organizations using zoo animals to exemplify a culture of creativity and innovation.

Whether the content of the stories are about the remarkable or the commonplace, they are all announced in such a way as to emphasize their interestingness to the audience. This is very apparent in the following example in which Tom Peters recounts his experiences of eating in an Italian restaurant in Auckland, New Zealand.

**Extract 6.1 – "Volarios Restaurant" [SwS: 00.05.50]**

Peters: You know I have been doing this for 25 years. I've got to admit that this is sort of one of my favourite stories ever. A while back, a year back roughly, I was visiting for the first time Auckland New Zealand. And by sheer accident we ended up next to an Italian restaurant.

In this preface Peters clearly announces that he is about to tell a story and then uses in the next sentence a temporal locator – "A while back, a year back roughly". The latter device is one commonly used by storytellers. Indeed, there are clear resonances between Peters' phrasing and the classic opening lines of many fairytales – 'Once upon a time. . .' – or folktales 'Long, long ago . . .'. The members of the audience are likely to be very familiar with these conventions and so can anticipate the commencement of a story. Audience attentiveness is further raised by Peters indicating the personal importance of this particular story. He states that of all the stories he has told in his long career as a public speaker that which he is about to tell is one of his favourites. Thus, the significance of this story is not simply that it is a good illustration of the point he has previously been developing (the importance of customer service), but rather that it also has special meaning for Peters. This is further highlighted by the additional emphasis on the phrase in lines 2 and 3 "my favourite stories ever". In prefacing the start of this story in this way Peters is likely to heighten the attention of audience members and give them an added incentive to listen to the story even more closely because they are about to share in something which is marked out as being very special to the speaker.

In the following example, Senge uses another type of story preface to illustrate his previous characterization of the American education system. He announces that he is about to tell a humorous third-party story, the source of which is the economist Fred Kaufman.

**Extract 6.2 – "Fred Kaufman" [FD: 00.04.40]**

Senge: Fred Kaufman used to tell a funny story about that.

In this extract Senge similarly explicitly declares that the next segment of talk is a story. This is very similar to saying "I am now going to tell you a story". Further emphasis is provided by his initial characterization of the story as "funny". This informs the audience of the nature of the climax of the story and the appropriate response expected when this point is reached. The distinctiveness of the story is additionally signalled because the source is a well-respected economist. Thus, in this short sentence Senge imparts a great deal of information to the audience. They know he is about to tell a story, that it is intended to be projected as humorous and that the source is an individual of high regard.

In a similar type of story preface the distinctiveness of a forthcoming story is emphasized by the gurus explicitly identifying from the outset the organization that is the subject of the story, as the following examples illustrate:

**Extract 6.3 – "Mister Gates" [LinL: 00.17.50]**

Hamel: A few days ago I was with some of the folks at Microsoft who are creating all of their online businesses. And Mister Gates came along and made kind of an interesting statement . . .

**Extract 6.4 – "Intel" [MC: 00.06.19]**

Kanter: And I told this story out in the Valley at a big meeting and a man came up to me from Intel and he said that on his first day on the job at Intel he came and there was a llama in the lobby.

In the first extract, Hamel indicates the onset of a story partly by the use of a temporal locator in that the events about to be recounted took place in the past. This is further emphasized by his stress on the word "few". In the second extract Kanter uses the same device as Peters in Extract 6.1 and Senge in Extract 6.2 by explicitly stating that she is about to embark on telling a story. Both

Hamel and Kanter further indicate that the sources of these stories are events that occurred while they were pursuing their professional activities (i.e. visiting organizations and giving public speeches). Their specialness derives from the fact that the subjects of the stories are identified at the outset. In these, and the other cases, the organizations identified as the subject of the forthcoming story are likely to be (1) familiar to the audience, (2) widely respected and (3) commonly viewed as successful at the time the story was told. During their talks the gurus do not refer explicitly to individuals and organizations that are likely to be unknown to the members of the audience or regarded as failures. Rather, they refer to organizations that can be immediately identified by the audience and are viewed positively.

Finally, the gurus formulate a transition to a story using a combination of the types of preface just discussed. Most commonly they demarcate a story by indicating that it is both particularly special to them and concerns a named person and/or organization. In the following example Kanter illustrates her previous point about the need for companies to draw from innovations outside of their normal areas of expertise and to quicken their decision-making processes by recounting a story of how a small company outflanked its much larger competitors:

**Extract 6.5 – "Ocean Spray" [GCBA: 00.21.15]**

Kanter: My favourite all time example of that is comes from a little company in Massachusetts, actually right near where I live, actually not so little anymore, called Ocean Spray Cranberries.

In a further example Kanter informs the audience that she is about to tell a story to illustrate her earlier point about the need to inform all employees, regardless of level in the organization, about the nature of the firm's strategy:

**Extract 6.6 – [GCBA: 00.07.45]**

Kanter: One of my FAVOURITE stories about that kind of system was told to me by Charlie Brown the late Chairman of AT&T, who was starting to see the need for change and trying to produce it in the early nineteen eightees.

In Extracts 6.5 and 6.6 the story is identified as one of Kanter's favourites. This is further emphasized by the additional stress on the word 'favourite'. The subject of both stories is also identified from the outset.

In summary, the previous discussion has shown that the gurus demarcate stories from the surrounding speech material by deploying a variety of story prefaces. While the events and happenings described within the stories in the great majority of cases are unremarkable, the preparatory work of the prefaces has the effect of increasing audience attention by signalling that something important, noteworthy or special is about to be told. Given that a lecture involves the guru speaking for an extended period of time, in this context story prefaces are not about increasing the chances of the speaker talking for more than one utterance, as they would be in normal conversation. Rather, story prefaces in public speaking appear to be primarily concerned with attracting, sustaining and increasing the attentiveness of the audience. As Atkinson (1984a, 1984b, 1986) notes, in any context where one person speaks for the great majority of the time the opportunities for others getting a turn to speak are limited. As a consequence, the incentives to pay close attention to what is being said are greatly reduced. Story prefaces increase the listenability of the next segment of talk by (a) highlighting their content from surrounding speech materials and (b) projecting a clear point for the onset of the story in question. In other words, they call attention to passages in the gurus' talks which the speakers identify as having significance and to which a particular orientation on the part of the audience is sought. In doing so they provide the audience with an increased incentive to listen to these parts of their talks. In this respect they are akin to rhetorical statements like contrasts, three-part lists and puzzle–solution formats which, as we have seen in Chapters 3 and 4, emphasize messages and provide audience members with resources that enable them to anticipate what a speaker is about to say.

One noticeable feature of the gurus' stories is that they contain a large proportion of the laughter that is generated in these lectures (72%). As we noted in Chapter 4, one way in which the gurus establish the relevance of audience laughter is through the use of a range of verbal and non-verbal actions during the delivery, and/or following the completion, of their messages. These include (1) announcing that they are about to say something humorous, (2) smiling or laughing and/or (3) using 'comedic' facial expressions, gestures and prosody. What we would like to suggest here is that story prefaces may foreshadow the deployment of these actions by elevating the incentives to listen. In doing so they channel and upgrade the audience's attention and in the process support and facilitate those actions that underpin the effective elicitation of laughter. In other words, they ensure that the audience is paying attention and so is more likely to notice and respond to those mechanisms that elicit a positive audience response, which in the context of these lectures is audience laughter. Given the large-scale nature of the events at which the gurus talk, in that many hundreds of people may be present, it is more difficult in these circumstances to secure and sustain the attentiveness of the audience members. Indeed, the audience may have difficulty seeing the speaker on the stage or as they move among the audience. While these problems are increasingly being overcome by the use of cameras that project images of the speaker to screens placed throughout the auditorium, they are of little help if the speaker does not gear their performances towards assisting the audience to remain attentive in the first place. In such large and non-intimate auditoria people's attention can easily wander as they lose focus on what a speaker is saying. Where laughter is present the stories may provide a moment in which the audience's attention is initially captured and focused prior to the speaker deploying a range of devices that encourage the audience to join in acts of collective affiliation. Although we are unable to categorically state that this is the case, this two-stage process of gaining audience attention (story preface then deployment of mechanisms that elicit laughter) may increase the likelihood that an invitation to laugh is accepted and results in collective laughter.

## The functions of the gurus' stories

Storytelling is clearly seen by the gurus as more than just a way of entertaining their audiences. As Kanter says in one of the extracts below "you will see my point in a minute, I'm not just trying to entertain you". The gurus do not present their stories as 'mere' entertainment. They indicate that the stories have a purpose. Indeed, they are intimately connected to the arguments and ideas they are presenting. Thus, they tell their stories in ways which indicate that, however whimsical they may appear at first sight, they have a serious point in respect of the gurus' management ideas and visions. However, their stories also have less visible functions. As we shall argue in this section, in addition to illustrating their ideas, the stories help bolster the authority of their knowledge claims and often exemplify their purported star status.

### *Illustrating and supporting gurus' ideas and visions*

All the gurus use stories to provide their audiences with concrete illustrations and support for their claims. They are intended to show their ideas in a good light. The stories therefore either praise those practices which they approve or disparage those that they regard as examples of bad management. Whichever type of story they tell our analysis indicates that the gurus tell their stories in two ways that have significance for the projection and reception of their core messages. In some cases the gurus adopt a three-part narrative structure in which they (1) begin by making an assertion that is clearly linked to the previous section of talk, (2) then substantiate the point by telling the story and (3) finally link the original assertion, prior talk and story together by summarizing and repeating an assertion they may have made in their preamble to the story. Thus, although the audience may have been aware of the point of the story, by repeating it after telling the story the gurus ensure that they are left in no doubt of the story's key message. By employing this structure the story is told in such a way that it raises the audience's attention through the story preface and then funnels this towards an explicit statement of the purpose or moral that is then linked back to point being developed in the prior talk. In this respect the story is fully integrated into the surrounding speech material. The following story told by Kanter illustrates this three-part narrative structure.

**Extract 6.7 – "Charlie Brown" [GCBA1: 0.07.45]**

RMK: Now there was a ti:me (.) when we didn't have to count o:n (0.5) people at the (.) lowest levels, at the grass roots, at the street level, at the production level to understand our policy or do anything about it. Because all they di:d was a narrow routinized job in which they had no decisions to make, (0.7) no autonomous actions, no power,=no influence, they did what they were told. (1.4) In fa:ct (1.0) that was the essence of bureaucracy, you don't have to know our strategy just do the job. (0.5) One of my favourite stories about that kind of system (0.4) was told to me by Charlie Bro:wn (0.7) the late chairman of ATT, who was starting to see the need for change and trying to produce it in the early nineteen eighties.=And so he visited a lot of the ATT factories. The telephone factories, (0.2) Western Electric was the division name. (0.5) And he talked about (0.5) chatting with a woman on the assembly line who thought she was making iro:ns. (0.4) She thought she worked for General Electric.

Audience: LLLLLLL (0.7)

RMK: The thing that was (.) amazing to him was that people (.) in order to do the jo:b people didn't have to know what product they made. (0.5) All

they had to do was follow instructions,=and do
their piece of the process. (0.5) Well toda:y (0.2)
People need to know the connection between
their activities and the overall focus, skills of the
fir:m.

In this story, she begins by asserting that lower level employees working in bureaucracies were once unaware of the strategy being pursued by the organization for which they worked (lines 1–11). She then announces the telling of a story, originally told to her by Charlie Brown, the former CEO of AT&T, and explicitly links this to the prior talk when she states that it is "One of my favourite stories about that kind of system" (lines 11–16). The story is clearly established from the outset as an exemplar of the point she has previously been developing. The story is then articulated (lines 16–22) and ends by emphasizing the key point that she wishes the audience to draw from the story, in this case all employees, regardless of their position in the organization, should be aware of its common values and goals (lines 24–31). In this instance, the end of story is delivered as a punch line to a humorous remark that elicits laughter from the audience. The summary following the story makes a contrasting point to the preamble. In the latter she states in lines 9–11 that bureaucratic systems support a view that "you don't have to know our strategy just do the job". She demonstrates the limitations of this approach by telling a humorous story that underlines the purported ridiculousness of this approach. Finally, she concludes by reiterating that "People need to know the connection between their activities and the overall focus . . . of the firm" (lines 29–31).

In other cases the gurus use a truncated, two-part structure in which the implication of the story, and its connection with prior talk, is revealed only after it is told. Thus, the reason for the story being interesting remains a mystery to the audience until it is revealed at the end. One danger with this approach is that the audience may wonder about the story's relevance to what has just been said with the consequence that their incentive to listen to the subsequent passage of talk is reduced. However, this story structure may overcome this potential difficulty by being presented in a puzzle–solution format. This may raise rather than reduce audience attentiveness. We have already discussed the nature of this rhetorical device in Chapters 3 and 4 in relation to elicitation of applause and laughter. Briefly, a puzzle–solution operates by establishing some kind of conundrum or dilemma in the minds of the audience and then, shortly afterwards, offers a solution to the puzzle that articulates and emphasizes the key message the speaker wants to get across. The following story is an example of this two-part structure.

**Extract 6.8 – "Mister Gates" [LinL: 0.17.50]**

GH: This is not just the glo:bal economy,=this is the
instantaneous eco:nomy. (0.5) And one of the
things that means is that the dividing line today
between leader and laggar:d is measured some-
times in months. (0.2) No longer in decades.
(0.2) er: It was a few days ago I was with some of
the folks at Microsoft who are creating all of
their o:nline businesses. .hhh And er Mister
Gates came along and made kind of an inter-
esting statement.=He said at Microsoft we are
always two years away from failure:. (0.2) Now
maybe this is just for the consumption of the US
justice department I dont kno:w.

Audience: LLLLLL[LLLL *(Very light)*

GH: [But if you have the closest thing to a
legal monopoly you can get on this planet and
you still worry about irrelevance that says
something for the rest of us I think. (0.5)
Because it's not only product life cycles that are
getting shorter it's strategy life cycles that are
getting shorter, (0.4) and a company is going to
have to be able to reinvent its concept of who it
is and what it is not once a generation but
perhaps every three or four years.

In lines 6 and 7 Hamel uses a temporal locator to announce the start of a story. However, the story is not integrated into the prior talk. It is disjunctive in that it is not immediately apparent what the relevance of Microsoft and Bill Gates are to his previous comments. In lines 15–24 he clarifies the purpose of the story and in the process links it back to his earlier argument in the story summary. Thus the beginning of the story is disjunctive in relation to the preceding speech material. This raises the potential question: 'What has this story got to do with this point?' The story ends on a punchline that elicits light laughter. As the laughter dies away Hamel clearly establishes the link between the story and previous argument. In this way he answers the earlier question and at the same time solves any puzzle in the audience's mind with respect to the purpose and relevance of the story.

In summary, by using the two-part structure the gurus add emphasis to their stories and enhance audience attentiveness by presenting them with a puzzle – why are they telling this story? How does it relate to what has just been said? What is the point of the story? What are the key learning point(s) that the gurus are seeking to illustrate? In doing so they are likely to keep the audience's interest until they offer answers to these questions. Furthermore, the anticipation of the solution to the initial puzzle by the audience provides a significant moment at which to make a major statement in relation to their ideas. By contrast, the three-part structure by itself contains little mystery. It does much of the work for the audience and perhaps provides less incentive to listen. The connection to prior talk is explained so that the purpose of the story is clearly understood from the outset. The story is then told and, if the audience are still in any doubt as to the reasons for its telling, the link to the earlier passage of talk is re-articulated. Consequently, when seeking to illustrate their ideas and visions the two-part puzzle–solution story structure offers the gurus a further opportunity to channel the audience's attention to a core focal assertion.

## *Legitimating knowledge claims*

In seeking to persuade managers of the superiority and necessity of their ideas gurus are confronted with a key difficulty. The fact that they lack a formal and authoritative body of knowledge leaves their statements and ideas vulnerable to active questioning and criticism by audience members [as well as by other established gurus, would-be-gurus, journalists and academics] (Alvesson, 1993; Clark, 1995; Clark and Salaman, 1998; Hucsynski, 1993; Jackson, 2001). Our analysis indicates that the gurus seek to establish the authority of their knowledge and claims by telling at least one story in each performance during which they position themselves as disinterested researchers undertaking fieldwork in organizations in order to learn directly from managers and organizations. Thus, they characterize their ideas and theories as being grounded in extant management practice. They present themselves as initially sceptical or bemused by the actions of managers and organizations until their underlying logic and rationale is revealed to them after discussion with the managers concerned. On the basis of these discussions they are willing to abandon any pre-conceptions that they may have had. Thus, their approach to research is not about applying a priori notions developed in another setting to interpretations of organizational phenomena. Rather, it is about establishing in the minds of the audience that their ideas are based on actual observation of effective management practice in action. Through this characterization the gurus enhance the credibility of their ideas with audiences of managers because they emphasize the practical foundations of their knowledge and at the same its purity. That is, it is free from conceptual and theoretical distortion. In a sense, the gurus present themselves as envoys from the 'front line'. They are simply reporting what they have seen.

In adopting this stance they run the risk of undermining their putative status as revered management thinkers because there is nothing particularly special in what they are doing. Their research approach is very ordinary and, if they had the opportunity, members of the audience could also visit organizations and talk to managers. Therefore, the guru has in some way to elevate what they have seen so that it becomes special and beyond the capabilities of audience members. They do this in a two-stage manoeuvre. First, they present an analysis that may redefine and reinterpret what they have seen. Thus, in telling these stories they give them an analytical spin that establishes both the guru's status and the uniqueness of their ideas from those of other gurus. Second, they then link their analysis to other examples. In other words, they seek to provide further justification for their ideas by drawing on other experiences or examples that substantiate what they are saying. Such linkages relate to the gurus' own unique experiences. These processes are evident in the following stories related by Kanter. This sequence of stories is particularly significant because she has told it over a 10-year period. Given that it continues to feature in her lectures it is likely that she feels it works well. It is therefore an appropriate example of effective storytelling.

**Extract 6.9 – "Seymour Cray and animal stories" [MC: 0.06.19]**

Seymour Cray, the great computer designer who founded Cray Research and is still involved under contract as their chief computer designer, did a striking thing to symbolize the need for fresh view points. Every year, he loved to sail, so every year he would build a sail boat and sail it all summer and then he would destroy it at the end of the summer. He wanted to send the message to people that we can always improve on what you're doing, and that it's only by destroying, which is a little radical, but at least challenging the past, that we can move forward into the future. And he continued to reinforce this theme with a series of symbols about challenging assumptions and stretching thinking like the parade of elephants on the beach. This took place in California by the way it's not the kind of thing we do in New England. First came the small elephant and it had a number painted on its side, it was the financial goal that was all they could make if they accepted current assumptions. Then came a bigger elephant with a bigger number, and then a gigantic elephant with a huge number. And he kept saying "see if we shake up our thinking who knows how far we can go. We're limited by today's patterns and our belief in them."

Well this elephant story began to take on a life of its own because I do spend a lot of time out Silicone Valley, often helping some of those entrepreneurial companies get a little bureaucratic discipline. And I started running across more elephants. First I was shown a picture of Ren Z. who was then President of Versatex, a Xerox subsidiary, riding on the back of an elephant down the main streets of Palo Alto with the Stanford marching band behind him. So I said, thinking I was being very funny, "this is interesting this is the second elephant I have run into out here do you have a renting elephant service in Santa Claire County?" And they said "yes". Talk about advances in transportation. They said yes Marine World in San Jose have been renting there animals to local companies. So I thought about that for a while and I could see in this new environment of cross pressures and everybody looking for new competitive advantages exactly how it happened. They were sitting around one day at Marine World at their assets utilization review meeting to see if they had any assets that were under-deployed and could be used for revenue enhancement, and somebody came up with the animals. Now if it had been in New England that person would never had dared speak up, but because it was California there they are making their animals a profit centre. Like the Toronto Zoo, by the way, which has been packaging fertilizer which they sell which has been contributed by the animals at the Toronto Zoo. The Bronx Zoo also has one like this on the market, I hate to say this out loud in front of several thousand people, but they do have it on the market under the brand name Zoo Doo. Well you will see my point in a minute, I'm not just trying to entertain you. Because one more round to the elephant. I then thought this was very very funny so added it to my repertoire, and I told this story out in the valley at a big meeting and a man came up to me from Intel and he said that on his first day on the job at Intel he came and there was a llama in the lobby. So I said perfect straight person, "Why a llama?" And he said, "Because they couldn't get an elephant though the door." I should have known. But why am I spending all this time telling you silly animal stories? What was I seeing? I was seeing in that part of the country, at that time, this was the early eighties, it was the hot bed of creativity, activity and innovation. More change was happening there, more change was starting there. They were the source of surprises, or our new opportunities as the case may be. But in that environment I was seeing a culture of play and irreverence. A culture where people had fun, had a sense of humour, and did silly things. And when I put that together with the scientific evidence on creativity I realized that that was exactly right because what is creativity but play and irreverence. It's playing with ideas, challenging old assumptions and irreverence against somebody's tradition. And so they were setting an environment where people were freer to come forth with new technological ideas, new serious ideas, because they were also freer to express other kinds of silly or crazy or wild ideas.

In these stories Kanter identifies herself as learning from her experiences while working with companies and talking to managers. She presents herself as initially perplexed when she encountered the elephants, but after discussions with managers their significance becomes apparent. The story is accompanied by a commentary that is not essential to the narrative but nevertheless presents Kanter's evaluations of the managers and organizations. With the phrase "What was I seeing?" she begins her evaluation and presents her analysis. This is not necessarily related to the managers' own views of what they were doing and also seeks to link the lessons from a number of different examples.

In summary, the gurus seek to establish the authority of their knowledge and claims by telling at least one story in each performance that is designed to establish the voracity and legitimacy of the ideas that they are communicating to audiences of managers. In telling these stories, the gurus position themselves as disinterested researchers learning directly from managers and organizations. The gurus present themselves as initially sceptical or bemused by the actions and situations they observe until their underlying logic and rationale is revealed to them after discussion with the managers concerned.

### *Enhancing the gurus' status*

The use of stories also enables the gurus to create impressions of their value and to enhance their putative star status. One fairly obvious way in which they do this is through using stories as an opportunity to name/refer to senior managers and large organizations that they have come into contact with. We can see this in a number of previous extracts in this chapter, for example in the sequence of stories above Kanter refers to Seymour Cray, Xerox and Intel. In other extracts she has referred to AT&T and Ocean Spray. In Extract 6.8 Hamel refers to Microsoft and Bill Gates. The gurus' lectures are replete with such references. Fincham (1995) has noted that gurus' books similarly abound with citations to managers and organizations. Apart from providing evidence for their claims and ideas, the deliberate naming of individuals and organizations that they have come into contact with also legitimates their message. In using these forms of citation the guru is attempting to benefit from the reputation of others by (1) demonstrating the breadth of their contacts and ready access to senior managers and organizations, (2) directly linking their ideas to people and organizations that the audience will respect and (3) demonstrating that people and organizations are already committed to and successfully using their ideas. The implication of this is that if these individuals and organizations that audience members hold in high esteem are successful doing what the guru identifies as necessary then so should they.

Additionally, they also tell stories which suggest that they are in constant demand, that they have a high market value, and that they are seeking to learn at every opportunity; no situation is too mundane. For example, this is very apparent in a number of stories told by Peters, in which he recounts personal experiences that substantiate the ideas he is advocating. In these stories he positions himself as an everyday member of the public. However, in all instances these experiences are presented as occurring while he was conducting his work as a guru. In the following example he recounts his experiences of staying in a hotel. He establishes in the first six lines that he stayed at the hotel while attending a conference, that it was large, glamorous and "glitzy", and that, while it was expensive, his stay had been paid for by the organizers of a conference. His star status is further emphasized by the fact that he stayed in a large suite on the top floor.

**Extract 6.10 – "Glitz and glimmer hotel" [TPE1: 0.19.00]**

Over a year ago I gave a seminar in Colorado and it was held in one of those marvellous new look hotels $150 million dollar monuments to glitz and glimmer, enough brass and marble to sink several battle ships. The people who put me up at this seminar were kind enough to put me in a big suite on the top floor of this hotel. It was a lovely suite, a most beautiful collection of fake antique furniture I have ever seen in my life. Now I will reveal to you two personal habits which are none of your darn business. Basically one of them is that I do my writing by getting up at four in the morning, and the second one is that if we had a physician at this conference he or she would probably be able to classify me as psychologically addicted to coffee. It is not that I like my caffeine but it's that I need my caffeine in the morning. So the first thing I look at when I get to any hotel is do they have all night room service – and this one did not. Bad enough that it had been $50 per night, but at $250 that's irritating. However, next to my bed on the bed stand was a listing of the usual services one finds in a hotel and it was entirely clear that room service begins at 6.15 in the morning. Fine and dandy I got up early the next morning to do my writing. Feeling in a particularly charitable mood I wait until 6.18 to call down stairs. When I call at 6.18/6.19 I get the tape recording message which says room service opens at 6.30. Now despite of all my commentary a minute ago, my addiction is not so great that in reality 6.15 versus 6.30 makes a great deal of difference to me – unless you promise me 6.15 and them I'm pissed. But the point I want to make, the next words I want to very clearly and rapidly utter is that I acknowledge that what I am saying is not fair, but I am the customer and that's the way I choose to make my judgement, and that's the way customers make judgements on things generally.

Stories such as this not only illustrate their ideas but they also enable them to enhance their status by among other things suggesting that they are in constant demand and that they have a high market value. By linking this to the earlier point that their lectures are full of references to individuals and organizations who are likely to be held in high regard by the audience, we can see that the gurus construct an image of themselves circulating with ease among some of the most successful business people and businesses in the world. In this respect, they appear part of the business glitterati or jet set. Furthermore, rather than foisting themselves upon this community, they are invited to participate and in turn are revered by those very groups and individuals that the members of the audience, and the wider community, are themselves likely to venerate. The lectures therefore celebrate and reinforce the star status of the gurus in a number of ways. The event itself involves considerable pre-publicity in which the virtues of the gurus' ideas and their influence and impact are vigorously sold. The venue is often a five star or landmark hotel in a key city. The auditorium is laid-out in such a way that the guru's status is further emphasized. Their face and name is often to be found on banners and the electronic backdrop. The delegate packs often contain branded badges, mugs, pens and copies of their latest book. And, as we have shown, segments of the talks themselves further enhance their star status. All of these factors combine to leave the audience in little doubt that they are attending a special event and listening to an exceptional talent. In the process the gurus' reputations are further embellished.

## Conclusion

Storytelling is a critical element of the gurus' public presentations. The use of stories is a central means through which the gurus seek to entertain their audiences and to some extent the people who attend these events expect to be entertained in this manner. However, as we have seen, the role of stories is not restricted to 'mere' entertainment. Critically, they are an important mechanism through which the gurus illustrate their key ideas and visions. In the process they make their ideas more immediate and show how they can work to the advantage of audience members. In terms of the activity of giving a public lecture, the way in which they are projected is a critical device for enhancing audience attentiveness. As we have shown, by using different types of story prefaces the gurus indicate both that they are about to tell a story and that it is significant, either for them or the audience. In this way, they announce the interestingness of what follows and so heighten audience attention in a context in which the incentives to listen are severely curtailed. Story prefaces therefore work in a similar way to the rhetorical techniques discussed in Chapters 2 and 3.

The stories also have more personal benefits in that they provide an opportunity for the gurus to establish the authority of their claims by demonstrating the factual basis of their ideas and their own unique insight. They are also a medium through which the gurus can establish their own status within the broader business community by associating their ideas with highly regarded, well-known and successful people and/or organizations. Thus, stories are central to establishing and reinforcing their claims to possess authoritative knowledge. In a market in which small differences in the perceived quality or utility of ideas is the difference between achieving guru status and striving for recognition, successful gurus have to constantly persuade the managerial audience of the continuing relevance and superiority of their ideas. Stories are a key way in which they achieve this in their live talks to managers.

Chapter 7

# Conclusion

In the 1980s Max Atkinson (1984a, 1984b, 1986) published a series of influential studies of political oratory, which provided unique insights into the ways Western politicians communicate their ideas and visions to domestic and international audiences, and explained why some politicians gain reputations as outstanding public speakers. By analysing video recordings of political speeches, Atkinson revealed that the elicitation of favourable audience responses, such as applause, depends on the use of a relatively small number of rhetorical devices, the mastery of which is associated with spellbinding oratory. He also suggested that these devices are not restricted to political oratory or to the elicitation of applause but have a powerful appeal when used effectively in a wide range of contexts where the aim is to persuade an audience. However, while several researchers have built on Atkinson's work, they have focused exclusively on various forms of political oratory, with the result that relatively little is known about whether and how the practices deployed by political speakers are used in other types of public speaking. This book has sought to address this limitation.

Our study supports Atkinson's thesis in that it shows that the techniques he identified are also used by another group of speakers whose professional success depends to a large extent on their ability to build personal reputations as powerful orators. As we showed in Chapters 3 and 4, the management gurus, like politicians, use these devices to highlight their core messages, regardless of whether they are inviting collective audience responses. They are thus an important structuring device for the speeches as whole and the communication of messages in general, whether audience response is sought or not. However, our study also reveals the importance of other presentational techniques that are of equal importance in the guru's armoury of oratorical skills. Many of these techniques are concerned with the evocation of laughter which, as we have seen, is the main form of collective audience response during the gurus' lectures.

Our analysis and discussion in Chapter 4 showed that episodes of collective audience laughter are not simply spontaneous reactions to messages whose content are self-evidently humourous, but rather are evoked by the gurus through the use of a range of verbal and non-verbal presentational techniques. These techniques include the verbal rhetorical devices discussed by Atkinson (1984a, 1984b) in his studies of applause and political oratory. However, our research also shows that even when the gurus *do not* package their messages in one or more of these verbal devices, their messages follow the same principles as those which involve their use. They, nonetheless, mark out messages from a background of other speech material and provide them with clearly projectable completion points around which audience members can co-ordinate their actions. In this way they package their messages in different ways to achieve the same ends. Audiences, if they are to respond on cue, need to know that and when it is appropriate to laugh.

In evoking laughter the gurus also deploy presentational techniques that are specifically associated with the generation of audience laughter. Rather than relying on audience members to recognize that laughter is relevant solely on the basis of the content of their messages, the gurus routinely use a range of non-verbal and, less commonly, verbal cues to signal their humorous intent. In this book we have seen that the practices the gurus use to signal humorous intent – facial expressions, exaggerated gestures, mimicry, etc. – can themselves provide sources of humour which are independent of the content of gurus' messages *per se*. This means that when the gurus use these techniques to signal their humorous intent, they render subsequent collective audience laughter ambiguous in respect of its relationship to the gurus' core messages. This is important because it allows speakers to elicit laughter in response to messages which convey their core ideas, without requiring audience members to engage in unequivocal expressions of agreement with the values embodied in those ideas. As we have seen, the gurus may also distance humour recognition from their core messages by inviting audiences to laugh at ancillary issues, such as unusual examples or outcomes of the practices they are recommending. Once again, laughter does not represent an unvarnished expression of support for the gurus' core ideas and visions. The gurus also achieve similar ends by articulating their views by reference to non-management contexts.

Our analysis shows how humour and laughter provide speakers and audiences with a flexibility that is perhaps absent in the case of applause. Unless it is used ironically or in conjunction with audience laughter, applause represents an unvarnished expression of support for the ideas expressed via precipitate messages (Clayman, 1992). In contrast to applause therefore, laughter provides a vehicle through which speakers and audiences can participate in affiliiative exchanges and, by extension, displays of group solidarity and cohesiveness, regardless of whether they agree on the core issues that are being addressed by the speakers. This is especially important in management gurus' lectures due to the nature of their audiences, which contrast sharply with modern day party political conferences in which very different conditions apply. Unlike speeches at party political conferences and rallies, management conferences and seminars are not generally comprised of a homogeneous audience who can be considered to share a similar point of view on a range of issues. Whereas open displays of disagreement were once tolerated, even expected, at party political conferences, more recently they have become carefully managed events that try to ensure a common and harmonious message is communicated. Gone are the days when a section of a political party would openly boo and heckle the party leader as they delivered their main conference speech. Political party conferences are now more sterile affairs in which delegates and speakers are corralled in such a way that they all remain 'on message' and criticism is confined to fringe meetings rather than the main auditorium. Indeed, access to the main auditorium is strictly controlled and limited to party members. Journalists and other interested observers are located in side rooms with a live feed from the conference floor. This eradicates the possibility that a television camera may inadvertently capture a response, given by a non-interested individual, that could be perceived as disaffiliate, such as a yawn or failure to clap at the right moment, or only half-heartedly. In these circumstances a speaker is articulating their values and vision to an audience that they know will agree with the substance of their message. As Atkinson (1984a, 1984b) and Heritage and Greatbatch (1986) have shown, the great majority of applauded messages at political conferences are confined to attacks upon an 'out-group' (i.e. opposition parties). These speeches reflect that most democratic societies operate within 'the overarching "us and them" framework of national party politics' (Heritage and Greatbatch, 1986: 120). Thus, while there is an asymmetrical discourse at the heart of political debate, conference speeches aim to articulate, reinforce and praise a particular set of policies. These speeches are about conveying messages that draw upon and invoke a unified and shared sense of the world; shared at least by those within the auditorium. In this respect, applause at these events can be viewed as an unambiguous agreement with the views expressed. According to Clayman (1992: 45), applause in the political sphere 'has affiliation as its sole objective and is thus a purified expression of support'. By contrast, while laughter does imply affiliation, it is more equivocal in that audience members may be 'laughing because they appreciate a good joke and not because they support the speaker' (p. 45).

Unlike speakers at party political conferences, management gurus cannot fully anticipate and control audience response since their audiences are much more diffuse in nature. As Goodwin (1986: 284) has pointed out 'The use of the single terms, such as "audience", to refer to all those who are witnessing a performance has the power to suggest that an audience is in some sense a single, homogenous unit.' Audiences and their members can differ significantly from one another in ways that are relevant to the performance they are witnessing. With respect to management gurus and their live lectures these differences partly relate to the national diversity of their audiences. Guru lectures are not confined to one country. Typically they talk to audiences in a range of countries that include, among others, America, Australia, Brazil, Canada, Germany, Great Britain, Mexico, New Zealand, Singapore and Switzerland. Those who attend these talks are also from a range of groups including governmental and non-governmental organizations, private and public sector organizations and various industry sectors. Furthermore, these events, unlike party conference and pop/rock concerts, are not characterized as gatherings of uncritical and adoring fans. Members of the audience are therefore not only numerous but also highly differentiated in terms of the levels of affiliation to the gurus' ideas that they bring to the lectures. A key problem for management gurus, if they are to maintain their star status and their reputations as highly effective public speakers, is to deliver a lecture that, while a particular course of action is advocated, does not alienate sections of the audience. This has to be achieved within a context of not knowing in advance the extent to which members of the audience are sympathetic to the points of view they express. The fact that many management gurus are able to attract large audiences, and maintain their reputations as highly effective public speakers over a long period of time, suggests that they package their messages in ways which are received positively and so do not result in a negative response from their audiences, and so undermine their reputations. Our analysis indicates that they achieve this by deploying messages that do not seek, in the main, unvarnished expressions of support for their core ideas and visions from the members of the audience.

The techniques through which they achieve this are not only exceptionally important to building and sustaining their reputations but may also support the transfer of knowledge. A number of writers have argued that at the heart of this process are ideas that are characterized by considerable 'interpretative ambiguity' (e.g. Kieser, 1997). The argument is that for an idea to gain mass appeal it must 'lend itself to various interpretations to stand a chance of broad dissemination' (Benders and van Veen, 2001: 38). Therefore those ideas that have a degree of fuzziness are better able to attract different communities. This is because they act as boundary objects and so are 'plastic enough to adapt to local needs and the constraints of several parties employing them, yet robust enough to maintain a common identity across sites' (Star and Griesemer, 1989: 393). Humorous episodes may be such boundary points in that, as we have argued, laughter encourages affiliation but this may occur for a variety of reasons. Some audience members may express their affiliation for the ideas being communicated and others for the humour and the way in which it is packaged. In this way, a variety of interests can be accommodated into a single affiliative moment. Any potential underlying differences are obscured by open displays of affiliation. Consequently, such episodes encourage or permit a high degree of inclusivity.

The guru's ability to generate collective audience laughter is also important with respect to audience attentiveness. As Atkinson (1984a, 1984b, 1986) notes, in any context where one person speaks for the great majority of the time the opportunities for others getting a turn to speak are limited. As a consequence, the incentives to pay close attention to what is being said are greatly reduced. Holding the attention of the audience is critical if a guru, like any other public speaker, is not to lose an essential part of their life-support system – their audience – and in the process the additional revenue earning activities that their talks can potentially generate (i.e. book sales, consultancy, further speaking engagements). If they are to be regarded as effective public speakers, gurus therefore have to construct their presentations in such a way that they attract and sustain the attention of audience members. Should the audience become distracted or fall asleep then they are likely to be thought of as a boring and ineffective speaker and their message will be lost. Laughter also plays an important role in this respect. As Atkinson (1984b: 11–12) has noted with respect to his studies of applause, collective activities like laughter 'can be used as a substitute mode of response by people who are deprived of any individual opportunity to speak. Such displays of approval provide audiences with an in-built incentive to pay attention very similar to that imposed by the possibility of having to speak next during an ordinary conversation'. Thus, the use of laughter overcomes two key problems faced by all public speakers in that it attracts and sustains audience attention and obtains their affiliation in a situation where one speaker speaks for an extended period of time. In this circumstance the audience has less incentive to listen and pay attention to what is being said. However, episodes of laughter provide evidence that the audience has been paying attention to the preceding passage of talk and that it has had a favourable impact. In this respect, laughter 'provides a powerful spur to continued attentiveness. This is because, as soon as members of an audience have laughed for a first time, they will start looking out for more fun and the chance to laugh again' (Atkinson, 2004: 33). People enjoy it and want to repeat the experience; it is infectious. After an episode of laughter they will listen more closely to what the speaker says waiting for the next cue, even if it does not come immediately.

We have also argued that story prefaces appear to be another mechanism for attracting, sustaining and increasing the attentiveness of the audience. They increase the listenability of a segment of talk by foreshadowing its interestingness. As we showed in Chapter 6, while the content of the stories may primarily concern ordinary everyday events, they are projected as special and worthy of close attention. In this way, the gurus channel the attention of the audience to a focal message, since the story often ends with a summary and link to the previous point. By increasing the incentives to listen they work in a similar way to the rhetorical techniques.

The presentational techniques discussed in this book are not unique to guru oratory in particular or public speaking in general; they are generic speaking practices deriving from ordinary conversation. Thus, for example, as Atkinson demonstrated, contrasts, three-part lists and the like are used in all forms of speaking (and writing), especially when people are seeking to persuade others. Similarly, conversation analytic studies of laughter in ordinary conversation indicate that people use and rely upon the same range of verbal and non-verbal practices as do the gurus in order to produce, recognize and co-ordinate humour-related actions. In particular, they show that although humour is sometimes depicted as a spontaneous reaction to humourous talk, in practice it is routinely invited by prior speakers through the use of a range of techniques, which enable them too indicate that and when it is appropriate for others to laugh. Moreover, respondents have at their disposal an array of practices through which they can produce, or decline to produce laughter and other humour-related responses (e.g. Gavioli, 1995; Glenn 1989, 1991/1992, 1995; Jefferson 1979; Jefferson *et al.*, 1987; Rutter, 1997).

The same applies in relation to other presentational techniques used by the gurus. Storytelling is obviously a pervasive aspect of human communication and is used in a wide range of contexts to, *inter alia*, substantiate the points people are seeking to get across to others, to establish the authority of speakers' claims, and to enhance a speaker's status at social gatherings. Similarly, people in a wide variety of settings may seek to deflect criticism away from the recipients of their talk in order to avoid offending or alienating them. In these respects there is nothing at all mysterious or esoteric about the techniques the gurus use. They are the very same techniques we all use in a wide variety of social contexts ranging from intimate fireside chats with spouses through animated discussions with friends to presentations to colleagues at work. What sets the gurus apart from less accomplished speakers is their ability to use these techniques *effectively* in public speaking contexts in which orators are communicating their ideas and visions to audiences that are often highly differentiated, and which may include many persons who adhere to different points of view. In other words, it is not the gurus' use of the techniques *per se* that sets them apart from less able public speakers, but their ability to deploy these techniques so as to enhance audience attentiveness, to maximize the likelihood of affiliative audience responses, and to make their messages arresting, memorable, and acceptable, etc. Whether or not the gurus ability to do this is innate or learnt through experience and/or coaching is a question that lies beyond the scope of this book. However, it is critical to their success on the international management circuit. This is not because it guarantees that they will either convert their audiences to their ways of thinking or reinforce the views of those who already agree with them. While gurus undoubtedly endeavour to build and maintain a band of followers, we would argue that still more important is their ability to maintain their star status on the management lecture circuit, so as to safeguard their revenues and ensure that they continue to get the exposure they need to disseminate their ideas. Their ability to deploy the generic techniques effectively is therefore critical to their success because it enables them to build and maintain their reputations as effective, striking and entertaining public speakers. Obviously, this is necessary if they are to fill the auditoriums in which they speak with audiences of managers who are willing not only to listen to what they have to say but also to pay handsomely for the privilege of doing so.

Appendix

# Glossary of transcription symbols

The transcription symbols are drawn from the transcription notation developed by Gail Jefferson. For details on this notation, see Atkinson and Heritage (1984).

| | |
|---|---|
| [ | A left bracket indicates the point at which overlapping talk begins. |
| ] | A right bracket indicates the point at which overlapping talk ends. |
| = | Equals signs indicate that different speakers' utterances are 'latched'. They also link continuous talk by a single speaker that has been distributed across non-adjacent lines because of another speaker's overlapping utterance. |
| (0.5) | Numbers in parentheses indicate the length of silences in tenths of a second. |
| (.) | A dot in parentheses indicates a gap of less than two-tenths of a second. |
| - | A dash indicates a cutoff sound like a guttural stop. |
| <u>word</u> | Underlining indicates some form of stress via pitch and/or amplitude. |
| WORD | Capital letters indicate talk that is spoken louder than the surrounding talk. |
| Wo::rd | Colons indicate prolongation of the immediately preceding sound. |
| . , ? | Periods, commas, and question marks are used respectively to indicate falling, non-terminal and rising intonation. |

| | |
|---|---|
| (word) | Parenthesized words indicate that the transcriber was not sure of what was said. |
| ( ) | Empty parentheses indicate that the transcriber could not hear what was said. |
| (( )) | Double parentheses contain transcriber's comments and/or descriptions. |
| .hhh | hs preceded by a period represent discernible inhalations. |
| hhhh | hs without a preceding period represent discernible aspiration. |
| LLLL | A string of Ls are used to indicate laughter. |
| L-L-L | Spasmodic laughter is indicated by a chain punctuated by dashes. |
| xxxxx | A string of xs are used to indicate applause (other conventions apply as for laughter). |

# Notes

## 1 Management gurus

1 Citation analysis is not without serious problems (Clark, 2004). Unless each article is read it cannot indicate whether the idea is central or peripheral to the main topic or whether it is referred to positively or negatively. Citation analysis is limited to the counts of references to an idea in selected sections of the print media, mainly leading academic journals, semi-academic journals and the popular management press. Such a method cannot determine the degree to which ideas are 'adopted' by organizations. Nevertheless, there is a tendency in the literature to assume that there is a symbiotic relationship between the pattern in the volume of discourse and trends in the adoption and rejection of ideas by organizations.

2 See note 1 for limitations of this data.

3 This is a very simplified view of the membership of the management fashion-setting arena. One of the authors has argued elsewhere that agents, book editors, conference organizers and ghost writers are also important members of this community (Clark, 2004).

## 4 Generating collective audience response

1 These occur in *Thriving on Chaos 1*, *Thriving on Chaos 3* and *Service with Soul* and are not included in Table 4.1.

## 5 The role of humour and laughter

1 There are no examples of gurus evoking laughter in response to messages which criticize products or services.

# References


Abrahamson, E. (1996) 'Management fashion', *Academy of Management Review*, 21 (1), 254–85.

Abrahamson, E. and Fairchild, G. (1999) 'Management fashion: lifecycles, triggers, and collective processes', *Administrative Science Quarterly*, 44, 708–40.

Alvesson, M. (1993) 'Organizations as rhetoric: knowledge-intensive firms and the struggle with ambiguity', *Journal of Management Studies*, 30, 997–1015.

Asch, S.E. (1951) 'Effects of group pressure on the modification and distortion of judgements', in J. Guetzhow (ed.) *Groups, Leadership, and Men*, Pittsburgh, PA: Carnegie Press, pp. 177–90.

Atkinson, J.M. (1984a) 'Public speaking and audience response: some techniques for inviting applause', in J.M. Atkinson and J. Heritage, (eds) *Structures of Social Action: Studies in Conversation Analysis*, Cambridge: Cambridge University Press, pp. 370–409.

Atkinson, M. (1984b) *Our Masters' Voices: the Language and Body Language of Politics*, London: Routledge.

Atkinson, M. (1986) 'The 1983 election and the demise of live oratory', in I. Crewe and M. Harrop (eds) *Political Communications: the General Election of 1983*, Cambridge: Cambridge University Press, pp. 38–55.

Atkinson, M. (2004) *Lend Me Your Ears: All You Need to Know About Making Speeches and Presentations*, London: Vermilion.

Atkinson, J.M. and Heritage, J. (1984) *Structures of Social Action: Studies in Conversation Analysis*, Cambridge: Cambridge University Press.

Barley, S.R., Meyer, G.W. and Gash, D.C. (1988) 'Cultures of culture: academics, practitioners and the pragmatics of normative control', *Administrative Science Quarterly*, 33, 24–60.

Baur, C. (1994) 'Management evangelists in showbiz arena', *Sunday Times*, 19 June.

Bedeian, A.G. and Wren, D.A. (2001) 'The most influential management books of the 20th century', *Organizational Dynamics*, 29, 221–5.

Benders, J. and van Veen, K. (2001) 'What's a fashion? Interpretative viability and management fashions', *Organization*, 8, 33–53.

Boden, D. (1994) *The Business of Talk: Organizations in Action*, Cambridge: Cambridge University Press.

Boden, D. and Zimmerman, D.H. (1991) *Talk and Social Structure: Studies in Ethnomethodology and Conversation Analysis*, Cambridge: Polity Press.

Boje, D. (1991) 'The storytelling organization: a study of story performance in an office-supply firm', *Administrative Science Quarterly*, 36, 106–26.

Brodine, R. (1986) 'Getting the applause', in R.M.B. Bosinelli (ed.) *US Presidential Election 1984: an Interdisciplinary Approach to the Analysis of Political Discourse*, Bologna: Pitagoria Editrice.

Bull, P.E. (1986) 'The use of hand gesture in political speeches: some case studies', *Journal of Language and Social Psychology*, 5 (2), 103–18.

Burrell, G. (1989) 'The absent centre: the neglect of philosophy in Anglo-American management theory', *Human Systems Management*, 8, 307–12.

*Business Week* (1995) 'Did dirty tricks create a best-seller?', *Business Week*, 7 August, 30–3.

Carson, P.P., Lanier, P., Carson, K.D. and Guidry, B.N. (2000) 'Clearing a path through the management fashion jungle: some preliminary trailblazing', *Academy of Management Journal*, 43, 1143–58.

Caulkin, S. (1997) 'Quirky common sense at $95,000 a day', *The Observer* (Business Section), 13 April, p. 14.

Champy, J. (1995) *Re-engineering Management: the Mandate for New Leaderhsip*, Collingdale, PA: Diane.

Clark, T. (1995) *Managing Consultants: Consultancy as the Management of Impressions*, Buckingham, UK: Open University Press.

Clark, T. (2001) 'Management research on fashion: a review and evaluation', *Human Relations*, 54 (12), 1650–62.

Clark, T. (2004) 'The fashion of management fashion: a surge too far?', *Organization*, 11 (2), 297–306.

Clark, T. and Greatbatch, D. (2002) 'Collaborative relationships in the creation and fashioning of management ideas: gurus, editors and managers', in M. Kipping and L. Engwall (eds) *Management Consulting: Emergence and Dynamics of a Knowledge Industry*, Oxford: Oxford University Press, pp. 129–45.

Clark, T. and Greatbatch, D. (2004) 'Management fashion as image-spectacle: the production of best-selling management books', *Management Communication Quarterly*, 17 (3), 396–424.

Clark, T. and Salaman, G. (1996) 'The management guru as organizational witchdoctor', *Organization*, 3 (1), 85–107.

Clark, T. and Salaman, G. (1998) 'Telling tales: management gurus' narratives and the construction of managerial identity', *Journal of Management Studies*, 35 (2), 137–61.

Clayman, S.E. (1992) 'Caveat orator: audience disaffiliation in the 1988 presidential debates', *Quarterly Journal of Speech*, 78, 33–60.

Clayman, S.E. (1993) 'Booing: the anatomy of a disaffiliative response', *American Sociological Review*, 58, 110–30.

Clayman, S. and Heritage, J. (2003) *The News Interview: Journalists and Public Figures on the Air*, Cambridge: Cambridge University Press.

Covey, S.R. (1989) *The Seven Habits of Highly Effective People: Powerful Lessons in Personal Change*, New York: Simon & Schuster.

Crainer, S. (1997) *Corporate Man to Corporate Skunk: the Tom Peters Phenomenon*, Oxford: Capstone.

Dobson, J.F. (1919) *The Greek Orators*, London: Methuen.

Drew, P. and Heritage, J. (1992) *Talk at Work: Interaction in Institutional Settings*, Cambridge: Cambridge University Press.

Drucker, P. (1974) *Management: Tasks, Responsibilities, Practices*, London: Heinemann.

Eliade, M. (1987) 'Shamanism: an overview', in M. Eliade (ed.) *The Encyclopaedia of Religion*, vol. 13, New York: Macmillan, pp. 201–8.

Ernst, B. and Kieser, A. (2002) 'In search of explanations for the consulting explosion', in K. Sahlin-Andersson and L. Engwall (eds) *The Expansion of Management Knowledge: Carriers, Flows and Sources*, Stanford, CA: Stanford University Press, pp. 47–73.

Fincham, R. (1995) 'Business process reengineering and the commodification of managerial knowledge', *Journal of Marketing Management*, 11, 707–19.

Fincham, R. (1999) 'The consultants' offensive: reengineering – from fad to technique', *New Technology, Work and Employment*, 14 (1), 32–44.

Freeman, F.H. (1985) 'Books that mean business: the management best-seller', *Academy of Management Review*, 10, 345–50.

Furnham, A. (1996) 'In search of suckers', *Fortune*, 14 October, 79–85.

Furusten, S. (1999) *Popular Management Books*, London: Routledge.

Gabriel, Y. (2000) *Storytelling in Organization: Facts, Fictions and Fantasies*, Oxford: Oxford University Press.

Garfinkel, E. (1967) *Studies in Ethnomethodology*, Cambridge: Polity Press.

Gavioli, L. (1995) 'Turn-initial versus turn-final laughter: two techniques for initiating remedy in English/Italian bookshop service encounters', *Discourse Processes*, 19, 369–84.

Gerlach, N. (1996) 'The business restructuring genre: some questions for critical organization analysis', *Organization*, 3, 425–53.

Gibson, J.W. and Tesone, D.V. (2001) 'Management fads: emergence, evolution, and implications for managers', *Academy of Management Review*, 15(4), 122–33.

Gill, J. and Whittle, S. (1993) 'Management by panacea: accounting for transience', *Journal of Management Studies*, 30, 281–95.

Glenn, P.J. (1989) 'Initiating shared laughter in multi-party conversations', *Western Journal of Speech Communication*, 53, 127–49.

Glenn, P.J. (1991/1992) 'Current speaker initiation of two-party shared laughter', *Research on Language and Social Interaction*, 25, 139–62.

Glenn, P.J. (1995) 'Laughing at and laughing with: negotiating participant alignments in conversation', in G. Psathas and P. Ten Have (eds) *Situated Order*, Washington DC: University Press of America.

Goffman, E. (1983) 'Felicity's condition', *American Journal of Sociology*, 89, 1–53.

Goldratt, E.M. and Cox, J. (1982) *The Goal: a Process of Ongoing Improvement*, Croton-on-Hudson, NY: North River Press.

Goodwin, C. (1981) *Conversational Organization: Interaction Between Speakers and Hearers*, New York: Academic Press.

Goodwin, C. (1986) 'Audience diversity, participation and interpretation', *Text*, 3, 283–316.

Grady, K. and Potter, J. (1985) 'Speaking and clapping: a comparison of Foot and Thatcher's oratory', *Language and Communication*, 5, 173–83.

Greatbatch, D. and Clark, T. (2002) 'Laughing with the gurus', *Business Strategy Review*, 13 (3), 10–18.

Greatbatch, D. and Clark, T. (2003) 'Displaying group cohesiveness: humour and laughter in the public lectures of management gurus', *Human Relations*, 56 (12), 1515–44.

Grint, K. (1994) 'Reengineering history: social resonances and business process reengineering', *Organization*, 1, 179–201.

Guest, D. (1990) 'Human resource management and the American dream', *Journal of Management Studies*, 27, 377–97.

Hamel, G. (2002) *Leading the Revolution: How to Thrive in Turbulent Times by Making Innovation a Way of Life*, Boston, MA: Harvard Business School Press.

Hamel, G. and Prahalad, C.K. (1994) *Competing for the Future*, Boston, MA: Harvard Business School Press.

Hammer, M. and Champy, R. (1993) *Reengineering the Corporation: a Manifesto for Business Revolution*, London: Nicholas Brealey.

Heath, C. (1986) *Body Movement and Speech in Medical Interaction*, Cambridge: Cambridge University Press.

Heath, C. and Luff, P. (2000) *Technology in Action*, Cambridge: Cambridge University Press.

Heirich, M. (1977) 'Changing heart: a test of some widely held theories about religious conversion', *American Sociological Review*, 83, 653–80.

Heritage, J. (1984) *Garfinkel and Ethnomethodology*, Cambridge: Polity Press.

Heritage, J. (1995) 'Conversation analysis: methodological aspects', in U.M. Quasthoff (ed.) *Aspects of Oral Communication*, Berlin/New York: Walter de Gruyter, pp. 391–418.

Heritage, J. and Greatbatch, D. (1986) 'Generating applause: a study of rhetoric and response at party political conferences', *American Journal of Sociology*, 92, 110–57.

Heusinkveld, S. and Benders, J. (2001) 'Surges and sediments: shaping the reception of reengineering', *Information and Management*, 38, 239–51.

Huczynski, A. (1993) *Management Gurus: What Makes Them and How to Become One*, London: Routledge.

Jackson, B.G. (1996) 'Re-engineering the sense of self: the manager and the management guru', *Journal of Management Studies*, 33 (5), 571–90.

Jackson, B. (1999) 'The goose that laid the golden egg? A rhetorical critique of Stephen Covey and the Effectiveness Movement', *Journal of Management Studies*, 36 (3), 353–77.

Jackson, B. (2001) *Management Gurus and Management Fashions*, London: Routledge.

Jackson, B. (2002) 'A fantasy theme analysis of three guru-led management fashions', in T. Clark. and R. Fincham (eds) *Critical Consulting: New Perspectives on the Management Advice Industry*, Oxford: Blackwell, pp. 172–88.

Jefferson, G. (1978) 'Sequential aspects of storytelling in conversation', in J. Schenkein (ed.) *Studies in the Organization of Conversational Interaction*, New York: Academic Press, pp. 219–48.

Jefferson, G. (1979) 'A technique for inviting laughter and its subsequent acceptance declination', in G. Psathas (ed.) *Everyday Language: Studies in Ethnomethodology*, New York: Irvington, pp. 79–96.

Jefferson, G., Sacks, H. and Schegloff, E.A. (1987) 'Notes on laughter in the pursuit of intimacy', in G. Button and J.R.E. Lee (eds) *Talk and Social Organisation*, Clevedon, UK: Multilingual Matters, pp. 151–205.

Kanter, R.M. (1985) *The Change Masters: Corporate Entrepreneurs at Work*, London: Allen & Unwin.

Kanter, R.M. (1989) *When Giants Learn to Dance: Mastering the Challenges of Strategy, Management and Careers in the 1990s*, London: Simon & Schuster.

Kanter, R.M. (1995) *World Class: Thriving Locally in the Global Economy*, London: Simon & Schuster.

Kanter, R.M. (2002) *Evolve: Succeeding in the Digital Culture of Tomorrow*, Boston, MA: Harvard Business School Press.

Kennedy, G. (1963) *The Art of Persuasion in Greece*, Princeton, NJ: Princeton University Press.

Kennedy, G.A. (1994) *A New History of Classical Rhetoric*, Princeton, NJ: Princeton University Press.

Kieser, A. (1997) 'Rhetoric and myth in management fashion', *Organization*, 4 (1), 49–74.

Lewin, K. (1951) *Field Theory in Social Science*, New York: Harper.

Lofland, J. and Skonovd, N. (1981) 'Conversion motifs', *Journal for the Scientific Study of Religion*, 20 (4), 373–85.

Lorenz, C. (1993) 'The *FT* review of business books', *Financial Times*, 22 June.

McIlvenny, P. (1996) 'Heckling in Hyde Park: verbal audience participation in popular public discourse', *Language in Society*, 25, 27–60.

Maynard, D.W. (1984) *Inside Plea Bargaining: the Language of Negotiation*, New York: Plenum.

Meyer, J.C. (1997) 'Humor in members narratives: Uniting and dividing at work', *Western Journal of Communication*, 61 (2), 188–208.

Meyer, J.C. (2000) 'Humor as a double-edged sword: four functions of humor in communication', *Communication Theory*, 10 (3), 310–31.

Micklethwait, J. and Wooldridge, A. (1996) *The Witch Doctors: What Management Gurus are Saying, Why It Matters and How to Make Sense of It*, London: Heinemann.

Morgan, N. (2001) 'The kinesthetic speaker: putting action into words', *Harvard Business Review*, April, 113–20.

Oliver, N. (1998) *Rational Choice or Leap of Faith? The Creation and Defence of a Management Orthodoxy*, Cambridge: Judge Institute of Management Studies Working Paper No. 7/98.

Parkinson, C.N. (1957) *Parkinson's Law: Or the Pursuit of Progress*, London: J. Murray.

Peters, T. (1987) *Thriving on Chaos: Handbook for a Management Revolution*, New York: Alfred K. Knopf.

Peters, T. (1992) *Liberation Management: Necessary Disorganization for the Nanosecond Nineties*, New York: Alfred K. Knopf.

Peters, T. (1994) *In Pursuit of Wow!*, London: Macmillan.

Peters, T. (1994) *The Tom Peters Seminar: Crazy Times Call for Crazy Organizations*, New York: Vintage.

Peters, T. and Austin, N. (1985) *A Passion for Excellence: the Leadership Difference*, New York: HarperCollins.

Peters, T. and Waterman, R. (1982) *In Search of Excellence*, New York: Harper & Row.

Psathas, G. (1995) *Conversation Analysis: the Study of Talk-in-Interaction*, Thousand Oaks, CA: Sage.

Puffer, S.M. (2004) 'Introduction: Rosabeth Moss Kanter's *Men and Women of the Corporation* and *The Change Masters*', *Academy of Management Executive*, 18 (2), 92–5.

Rutter, J. (1997) *Stand-Up as Interaction: Performance and Audience in Comedy Venues*, unpublished Ph.D thesis, University of Salford, UK.

Ryave, A.L. (1978) 'On the achievement of a series of stories', in J. Schenkein (ed.) *Studies in the Organization of Conversational Interaction*, New York: Academic Press, pp. 2113–32.

Sacks, H. (1995) *Lectures on Conversation*, Oxford: Blackwell.

Sargant, W. (1997 [1957]) *Battle for the Mind*, Cambridge: Malor (1st edn. 1957).

Scheidel, T.M. (1967) *Persuasive Speaking*, Glenview, IL: Scott Foresman.

Senge, P. (1990) *The Fifth Discipline: the Art and Practice of the Learning Organization*, New York: Doubleday.

Senge, P.M., Kleiner, A., Roberts, C.B., Roth, G. and Ross, R.B. (1999) *The Dance of Change: the Challenges to Sustaining Momentum in Learning Organizations*, New York: Doubleday Century.

Senge, P.M., Roberts, C.B., Ross, R.B., Smith, B.J. and Kleiner, A. (1994) *The Fifth Discipline Fieldbook: Strategies and Tools for Building a Learning Organization*, New York: Doubleday Century.

Sharpe, T. (1984) 'The day I saw John Fenton or "By an Inch It's a Cinch"', *Management Education and Development*, 15 (1), 14–16.

Simmel, G. (1902) 'The number of persons as determining the sociological form of the group', *American Journal of Sociology*, 12, 23–53.

Sloan, A.P. (1964) *My Years with General Motors*, London: Sidgwick and Johnson.

Spell, C. (1999) 'Where do management fashions come from, and how long do they stay for?', *Journal of Management History*, 5, 334–48.

Spell, C. (2001) 'Management fashions: where do they come from, and are they old wine in new bottles?', *Journal of Management Inquiry*, 10, 358–73.

Star, S.L. and Griesemer, J.R. (1989) 'Institutional ecology, "translations" and boundary objects: amateurs and professionals in Berkeley's Museum of Vertebrate Zoology, 1907–39', *Social Studies of Science*, 19 (3), 387–420.

Suddaby, R. and Greenwood, R. (2001) 'Colonizing knowledge: commodification as a dynamic and jurisdictional expansion in professional service firms', *Human Relations*, 54 (7), 933–53.

*The Economist* (1994) 'Tom Peters, performance artist', *The Economist*, 24 September, 101.

Thompson, J.B. (1990) *Ideology and Modern Culture: Critical Social Theory in an Age of Mass Communication*, Cambridge: Polity Press.

Trapp, R. (1995) 'The gurus we worship in the workplace', *The Independent*, 18 August, 15.

Travisano, R. (1970) 'Alternation and conversion as qualitatively different transformations', in G.P. Stone and H. Faberman (eds) *Social Psychology Through Symbolic Interaction*, Waltham, MA: Ginn-Blaisdell, pp. 594–606.

Treacy, M. and Wiersema, F. (1995) *The Discipline of Market Leaders: Choose Your Customers, Narrow Your Focus, Dominate Your Market.* New York: Perseus.

Watson, T. (1994) 'Management "flavours of the month": their role in managers lives', *International Journal of Human Resource Management*, 5, 893–909.

Whyte, W.H. (1957) *The Organization Man*, London: Jonathan Cape.

Zimmerman, D.H. (1988) 'On conversation: the conversation analytic perspective', in J. Anderson (ed.) *Communication Yearbook 11*, Beverley Hills, CA: Sage.

# Index